there's a ghost in my room

there's a ghost in my room

living with the supernatural

SANJOY K. ROY

HarperCollins *Publishers* India

First published in India by HarperCollins *Publishers* 2025
HarperCollins *Publishers* India, Cyber City, Building 10-A,
Gurugram, Haryana – 122002, India
www.harpercollins.co.in

2 4 6 8 10 9 7 5 3 1

P-ISBN: 978-93-6989-632-5
E-ISBN: 978-93-6989-676-9

Typeset in 12/16.2 Adobe Caslon Pro at
HarperCollins *Publishers* India

Printed and bound at
Replika Press Pvt. Ltd.

This book is produced from independently certified FSC® paper to ensure responsible forest management.

*

HarperCollins Publishers, Macken House, 39/40 Mayor Street Upper, Dublin 1, D01 C9W8, Ireland

To Puneeta,
Aditya and Avik

Contents

Author's Note

There's a Ghost in My Room

My father, a sceptic, acknowledged Ma Durga and the many deities in the Hindu pantheon but didn't quite know what to do when it came to religion and ritual. It was my mother who was the family druid, having grown up in a home steeped in superstition that boasted of a 300-year-old family deity.

My childhood years were spent playing with gods and goddesses, immersing myself in family rituals, conjuring up bhog and putting the gods to sleep at night in their own tiny beds. As I grew older, I became, like Pa (my father), more of a sceptic than a believer. The death of a favourite dog had me move away from the notion of God completely, only to return to the acceptance of a higher universal energy in later years—once I sorted out my 'antenna', guided in part by Puneeta's belief in universal energy and that of an ascended master, Gurudev.

When preparing my horoscope, the family pandit had predicted that I would grow up to be a priest or a lawyer, which seemed mostly acceptable to my family who were indulgent of my spiritual bent of mind. As it turned out, neither prediction was borne out by reality. I did study law for five semesters, thanks to notes by Shobha Agarwal and tutorials by Sruti 'Tina' Kumari who primed me for the exams, but during one of the tests, I needed to take a dump and the choice was between the Law Faculty loo, which was beyond horrific, or the washrooms of the Oberoi Maidens. Maidens won, and that put to rest the idea of my becoming a lawyer.

The universe is an enigma. We know very little about the world outside and even less about our own abilities to communicate with the other world; but ESP is a reality, as is the notion of sixth sense or instinct. It's instinct that has led me to take most of my decisions: from making friends and engaging in relationships to working with business partners and accepting projects—and sometimes saying a firm 'no' to what appeared to be 'a once-in-a-lifetime opportunity'.

In most cases, these decisions have stood me in good stead!

Over the years, the paranormal has blended into our lives, enhanced by Puneeta's own experimentation with the occult and her understanding of healing energies. I have seen, sensed and interacted with otherworldly forces and have encountered the supernatural in many forms: spirits, spooks, eerie presences, an oppressive feeling of dread, a premonition, as well as being protected from many a danger by the unknown.

Spooks don't necessarily jump out at you in the most expected of places. I haven't chanced upon a ghost or a ghoul in the Valley of the Kings or Queens, in the Pyramids of Giza, at the Temple of Thebes or the caves of Cappadocia, but I have experienced them in more ordinary settings: in a vacant plot of land, on a tree outside the bedroom window, at home or on a riverbank. While I pretend to take these in my supposedly cool stride, I still jump out of my skin in terror when faced with an unexpected and uninvited apparition. For the most part, I am uncomfortable with the messages that I receive from the universe, which I am expected to convey to unsuspecting folks.

My stories are my reality—or certainly an interpretation of events that Puneeta and I and our larger circle of family and friends have experienced. How much has been reimagined from our peculiar perspectives is difficult to say. What I do know is that through the good and the bad, the horror and the madness, we have ultimately always felt protected, be it by the handprints of our spirit guides who are there to reassure us, or by the positive energy that abounds around us.

I am neither a soothsayer nor am I steeped in the occult; I do not predict people's future or delve into their past; I am neither mystic nor sceptic. And so, as you journey with me through time and place and through different dimensions, I leave you to draw your own conclusions, with the hope that when you look around you will realize that we don't quite have an understanding of the many dimensions we inhabit and that in living our lives we should embrace the miracles that happen around us every day and be grateful for what we have.

1

The First Haunting

Gooptu Baari, Calcutta

It was 1967; I was five years old. The news came that my Dadubhai (my mother's father) had suddenly passed away. My mother took the next available flight to Calcutta, albeit one that would take her on a circuitous route, while Probir, my elder brother—Dada, as I called him—and I accompanied our father a few days later by train. All packed, we headed to the station to claim our first-class carriage which had been cleaned and sanitized by the household staff for the long soot-encrusted journey that lay ahead: from Cochin to Calcutta via Madras.

Every year, we used to look forward to our summer holidays which meant visiting our grandparents' home in Calcutta, and the excitement of a second visit within a few months, despite the circumstances, was quite heady. Trunks, holdalls and suitcases were brought out; koraishooti'r kochuri (pooris stuffed with peas) were fried and packed into large tiffin carriers along with alur dom, fried bhindi, mango pickle, and food for Choppy, our Pomeranian whose sole mission in life was to rush into our room early in the morning, jump on the bed and tug at our pyjamas till we tumbled out and played with him.

My father, the legendary Mihir 'Micky' Roy of the Royal Navy, had trained at the Royal Military Academy at Dartmouth, served on a minesweeper and then on the HMS *York* before transferring to the Indian Navy in 1950 following Independence. He was a naval aviator and the first commander of the elite INAS 310 Squadron, nicknamed 'the Cobras', which flew the Bréguet 1050 Alizé anti-submarine warfare aircraft. He had trained in Hyères–Toulon in France to bring these aircrafts onboard the INS *Vikrant*, India's first aircraft carrier, and, having survived two crashes, headed back to India. He was now the commander of the INS *Garuda* naval base in Cochin.

We lived in Garuda House, a sprawling bungalow located in Fort Cochin on the backwaters, with a large silver oak tree from which the staff had constructed a swing for Dada and me to play on. Red ants inhabited the roots of the tree, and Dada, who loved experimenting with anything handy, used to add ants to a mixture of jam, coffee powder, honey and Bovril laced with Tabasco, melted Mars bars and black pepper, and offered up the concoction for me to taste. In many ways that prepared me for my later adventures with food and set the tone for tasting anything that came my way: from snake and fruit bat to deep fried cockroach wings and smoked worms! Dada was by far the more intelligent of the two of us. He was born in London, so we used to tease him as being Breeteesh!

Train rides meant an endless supply of food and drink, sticking your head out of the window, watching the coal engine spout steam, counting the coaches as they gently curved round a bend, and waving at carts and bikes, cars and scooters waiting at railway crossings. We travelled through the verdant countryside of southern India, over hills and through forests, across vast stretches of paddy fields and palm trees, watched over by our parents and the staff, who at each station would rush from their carriage to our compartment—which in those days was like an independent suite opening directly onto the platform—feed us, hastily wipe the soot off our faces and then race back to their berths before the train pulled out. Village kids ran alongside the tracks as the train whistled and puffed its way to Madras, where our bogies were unhitched from the coal-fired steam engine and parked on a side track, waiting to be attached to the next train that would take us to Calcutta.

Ready for the city, our faces scrubbed, our clothes changed, we would lean out of the window to see who could catch the first glimpse of Howrah Bridge, towering in the distance, heralding the end of our journey. The black Studebaker or the cream Dodge would be parked right by the platform at Howrah Station; it was always a wonder to see the car drive straight to the platform and pull up outside our compartment, waiting for us to alight.

The drive to No. 7 Gooptu Lane in Jorasanko was a short one, depending on the traffic on Howrah Bridge. Horn blaring, the car would weave its way in fits and starts through the crowd: countless porters, then called 'coolies', running to deliver their loaded wicker baskets balanced expertly on their heads, dhoti tied around their waist, their spindly legs showing; the endless procession of hand-pulled carts laden with fresh vegetables and spices, fish and poultry brought in from the surrounding villages by the local trains and being rushed to the market; hand-drawn rickshaw pullers with passengers perched precariously at the edge of sweat-infused red rexine seats, clinging for dear life as they snaked their way across the bridge, swerving between truck and tram, car and animal. For a kid, this chaos was all one could hope for in a big city, a rush of images and the giddy smell of life. It was enthralling.

Jorasanko was amongst the oldest neighbourhoods of north Calcutta and was home to a now fading aristocracy. The Jorasanko Raj Bari, with its fading polished red floors and white pillars, and the Thakur Bari, the Tagore homestead, were a stone's throw from Dwarkanath Gooptu's company headquarters. As the car turned into Gooptu Lane, we narrowly missed a squad of thelawallas who had chosen that moment to squat and pee while the darwan shouted at them to stop mid-stream and move, annoyed that the freshly painted walls were being violated just as the baba log were entering. Though the pungent smell of urine invariably had us gagging as we turned into the lane and drove up to the porch, our attention was caught by a bevy of cousins, uncles and aunts, waving enthusiastically from the gaadi veranda (the long balcony above the horse stables and the car garage) that ran along the length of the palace. The veranda had beautiful wrought-iron filigree railings; Dada had once pushed his head through them and been unable to get it out, creating total panic in the family.

Gooptu (from the anglicized pronunciation of Gupta or Gupto, the Bengali version dutifully rounded off with an 'O') Bari was built by Dwarkanath Gooptu, my great-great-great grandfather, in the mid-1800s. His father, Brindaban Chandra Guptoo, was one of the principal zamindars of Calcutta and had owned vast tracts of land in the then newly minted city, which became the capital of the East India Company and, later, the British Empire.

Dwarkanath Gooptu, along with Debendranath Tagore (Rabindranath's father), was educated in Hare School and was the favourite pupil of its founder, David Hare. At a time when the children of most zamindars were expected to be tutored at home and spend their days playing, hunting and fishing or, as they grew older, in the naach ghors or the halls of entertainment in their palaces, or away at their bagan baris or garden estates located along the river, going to school and receiving a formal education was a novelty, if not a middle-class pursuit to be avoided at all costs.

In 1835, when the Medical College of Bengal was formed, Dwarkanath Gooptu was one of the first four students admitted and he went on to assist Madhusudan Gupta in conducting the first human dissection in Asia. Upon completing his medical studies in 1839, he was offered a position as a doctor in the Northeast—which he declined—and instead set up a private practice, becoming the official physician to the Tagores and other zamindars and princely families of Calcutta. In 1840, Messrs D. Gooptu & Co. was registered as the first dispensary of English drugs in India to be run by a Bengali. The firm's first and most successful patent was the D. Gooptu Tonic which proved effective in fighting malaria and was prescribed widely across Bengal. Dwarkanath's proximity to the British (and their acknowledgement of the efficacy of the tonic) brought about exports to Africa and the Far East. The company went on to patent medicines for the spleen and liver, a tablet for diarrhoea and dysentery, and liver-purging pills. Each was hugely valued across the subcontinent and Africa, making Dwarkanath one of the most prosperous businessmen of his time. Wealth poured into the family vaults: carts laden with silver and gold coins carried in large wicker baskets were washed and sprinkled with Ganga jal on the instruction of the boro ginni, or the presiding lady of the house, before being laid out to dry in the uthon or the courtyards and vast interlinked terraces of the palatial residence that was spread across a whole city block and home to the ever-expanding Gooptu tribe.

When Dwarkanath Gooptu died in 1882, he left his laboratory and property to his three sons who, in turn, diversified and went on to patent other medicated and household products, including the F.N. Gooptu pencil and pens. Their landholdings multiplied and each brother and their families built magnificent mansions appointed with the finest Italian marble, chandeliers imported from Europe and Italian marble statuary that adorned staircases and hallways. Gold bathroom fittings and the best of European furniture were opulent sentinels to the esoteric tastes of this wealthy ruling class.

The third generation, fattened on their existing wealth and luxury, was less fortunate. My grandfather's uncle, Tarok Nath Gooptu, loved gambling and managed to run through the family fortunes, mortgaging no less than seventeen palaces in the prime areas of Calcutta to cover his betting debts. Each time his siblings confronted my great-grandfather and begged him to disown their brother, they were told that theirs was a respected founding family of Calcutta and that they should stand together in good and bad times; no member of the family would ever be disowned or be allowed to be sent to jail.

Eventually, Nos. 7 and 8 Gooptu Lane were the only properties remaining with this branch of the family tree as the others had moved to central and south Calcutta and built new residences in Middleton Street, Grey Street, The Strand and Rashbehari Avenue.

Despite the fickle fortunes of their ancestors, my mother and her brother led protected lives as children. She was driven to school every day in either the Standard or Rover cars, and was accompanied by a member of the household staff who would shepherd her to the gates, being extra protective in case a passerby gave her the evil eye. Her uncles spent their days playing cricket on the vast terraces that linked the many courtyards of the house. They wore blazers with their team colours emblazoned on the pockets. Their wives cooked up lavish lunches and dinners: ilish maacher jhal, shukto, kosha mangsho, murgi and chatni, muri ghonto and begun bhaaja, chingri and kakra were served up with melt-in-your-mouth luchis. No meal was complete without mishti doi and the freshest sandesh made by the family's mishtiwalla. Not surprisingly, many of them dropped dead in their forties and fifties, felled by coronary failure brought about in equal parts by their unhealthy lifestyles and a degree of boredom that passed off as the 'good life'. Like most zamindars, they lived off the rents from their estates and rarely looked to work. My mother's boro and choto pishis were married to men who were expected to move into the house and live as ghor jamais. My granduncles and grandaunts, and their children and grandchildren were ruled over by my great-grandmother, Didanu, with an iron fist; everyone was terrified of her and pandered to her every whim and fancy to keep her in good humour. Her room on the top floor, with its large four-poster bed, doubled as a throne room to receive guests as much as to pass judgement on all things that were brought to her notice by a bevy of servants and confidants who played one member of the family against the other.

As we alighted at the porch that day in 1967, we were greeted by Dubeyji, the household's trusted guard, whose domain was the rock platform at the entrance of the house, emblazoned with the D. Gooptu coat of arms and family seal. From here he negotiated with the daily traders and kept an eye on the goings-on of the household's many servants. We were immediately whisked off to the lal ghor, the red room—a vast, mostly empty space with wooden benches where Chotu napit (the family barber) waited to give us our customary haircuts. It was an endless battle to keep him from shaving our heads completely. His signature style was the baati chhaant or bowl cut, which he executed with great precision. One by one, we were plonked into a tall chair even as we wailed and flailed to little avail. Next was a hot bath to wash away the soot and, I suspect, to purify us, given the amount of Ganga jal that was mixed into the water. Then we were taken upstairs, past brooding portraits of our forefathers seated in gilded chairs set against satin curtains and peering at us quizzically from the ornate frames, to offer our condolences to our great-grandmother. Didanu lay propped up in her four-poster bed with the room's massive chandeliers dimmed and the mirrors covered with white sheets. A retinue of servants bustled about, massaging her legs, arranging her paan or adjusting the giant pillows and the pashbaalish (bolsters) and handing her an endless stream of clean linen hankies trimmed with lace to cry into each time a visitor approached to commiserate with her.

Didanu had loved my grandfather, her eldest son, and doted on my grandmother, her eldest daughter-in-law, and her very fair and beautiful granddaughter. A foot ladder was on hand for us to climb onto the majestic bed which was at a height well beyond our reach. She looked us up and down, kissed us on our foreheads, announced that we were thin and needed to be fed, and then proceeded to loudly weep and remonstrate with God about not being taken away instead of her beloved son.

We were then ushered downstairs to console Didibhai, my grandmother, whom we loved dearly. As we walked down the black-and-white chequered marble floor, the exotic macaws, Chinese cockatoos and the many budgerigars that were housed in cages along the length of the corridor greeted us with a 'boka chhele' (silly boy) or 'paaji chhele' (naughty boy) or a cackle, depending on their mood and whom they were imitating. The grandfather clocks, timed a second apart from each other, began to chime like a veritable concert of clocks, the sound following us from room to room, marking the passage of time and the passing of a gentle soul.

Didibhai was surrounded by her sisters-in-law and her extended family. She had been shorn of her jewellery and dressed in a starched white sari with a light grey border. Married at a very early age by her zamindar mother and eminent lawyer father, she still looked young and beautiful at forty, not yet ready to take on a new role bereft of the husband who had loved her deeply and live the life of a widow. Our grandfather, Dadubhai, wearing a white kurta with diamond buttons and sporting a Rolex watch and a gold-embossed ring with the family seal, stared out of a black frame, lifeless, warmed only by the pale flickering light of a diya reflecting off the glass.

We were passed from lap to lap as grandaunts and aunts ruffled our freshly cut hair, pinched our cheeks and kissed us on our foreheads, embracing us in a way only family can. The smells of camphor and jobakusum hair oil, mingled with rajnigandha flowers, carbolic soap and perhaps a hint of jasmine, lingered in the air.

Our holidays were spent exploring the length and breadth of the house, running to the apartments scattered across the many courtyards, peering in to see what was being cooked or what churan, achaar or aamshotto (dried mango set in layers) stored in large porcelain jars we could savour. We would scramble up the stairs to the terrace to play with our cousins, or dash off on adventures, looking for lost treasures or yet to be discovered rooms, secret passages and forgotten doors. The oldest part of the house, recessed at the back, which had once served as the kitchen and outhouse, was our favourite spot. Now mostly empty, it had the odd teak cupboard and discarded furniture covered in dust and cobwebs, which we could hide behind. Old writing tables with shuttered covers that had been tossed away by their owners still guarded the contents of their drawers and creaked wearily when probed, waiting to be restored, hoping for their patina to be polished with oil till they glistened in the light of the lamp and were once again trusted as keepers of gossip and family secrets. The cavernous rooms with their red polished floors edged with mosaic and tall wooden shuttered windows painted green, which hadn't been opened since our last visit, begged to be dusted and aired. This was our world, where we kids ruled.

We would play darkroom and when it wasn't dark enough, blindfold ourselves and hide in improbable spaces, inside cupboards and under dusty beds, leaping out with shrieks and war cries. We had legendary pillow fights and indulged in endless rounds of 'L-O-N-D-O-N—London, Stop!' where we had to freeze and not laugh, no matter the provocation, or we would be declared 'out'. Hours passed thus, the games ending only when we heard the household staff hollering at us to return to the main house for the hundredth meal of the day or to say hello to a visiting aunt, uncle or house guest. Even as we laughed and shared stories as we headed back, I would linger awhile to absorb the strangeness of this part of the house. Legend had it that during the many riots that had plagued Calcutta through its turbulent pre- and post-Partition history, people saved from the mobs were hidden here as it was almost impossible for an outsider to find their way around the house. This part of the house also had a reputation for being haunted.

According to family lore, a thief once broke into the thakur ghor, the family prayer room at No. 8 Gooptu Lane, the house built to entertain the burra sahib or the Britishers. Situated on the top floor of the mansion and adjoining the terraces, the cool, spotless black-and-white marble floors glistened at all times, reflecting the oil lamps that were lit through the day until it was time for the gods to retire for the night. They were laid to sleep in their miniature four-poster beds, their jewellery and crowns removed, their rich gowns changed for soft muslin, and the mosquito net rolled down; they were tucked into bed with a glass of water and small brass plates of fruits and sweets, just in case they woke up and were hungry. The thief, lured by stories of the fabled jewellery of the gods—diamond and ruby diadems, necklaces studded with emeralds and precious stones, and the gold and silver thrones that were housed in the room—had jumped terraces, clambered in through a window and tried to wrestle open the safe, only to find the windows and doors shutting around him on their own. He was found the next morning, terrified, pleading to be let out, and readily confessed to his crime.

Legend had it that Dwarkanath Gooptu's ancestors in the early eighteenth century, had had the same dream each night for a week, in which Goddess Durga asked to be retrieved from a pond on the estate. When the pond was drained, a bundle wrapped in a red cloth was found in the clay, and within it were idols of Durga, Ganesh and Kartik, made of ashtadhatu, an amalgamation of eight metals. These, along with Narayan, the isht devata or family deity, continue to be worshipped in a recently acquired temple in north Calcutta.

Over the years there had even been sightings of the goddess in the thakur dalan (the veranda outside the thakur ghor). During the early twentieth century, a fruit seller came to the residence asking to be paid for some aamra, or hog plums, that had been bought by a young girl in a red-bordered sari. The guards checked with the household staff and found no such person among them, and the women of the house never stepped out to deal with vendors. The next morning, when the priest opened the doors of the thakur ghor he found a peeled half-eaten aamra lying on the shinghashon (throne) of the goddess.

My aunt Indrani Gooptu, or Bouma as I called her, had on many occasions woken to the sound of the dhaak (drums) and the kashar ghonta (brass cymbals) and found the thakur dalan lit in a luminous golden hue. Once, she dreamt that the goddess asked for a pair of anklets. She immediately ordered a set and presented it to Gopal thakur, the head priest, who tied them around the goddess's feet. Each night when he put the gods to sleep, he would take off their jewellery and remove the anklets before tucking them into bed, a custom that is observed even today. One night, Bouma heard the tinkling of bells outside her room. She dismissed it as a figment of her imagination but shared the incident with the priest the next morning. That was when he realized that he had forgotten to take the anklets off the goddess's feet the night before. Opening the door of the thakur ghor, he found one anklet lying at the foot of the bed and another under the sheets, as if the goddess had shaken them off during the night.

Late in the evening, the thakur dalan and its courtyard lay silent with a sole diya lit to mark the passing of my grandfather. The chandeliers had been dimmed, the relatives had left and the family members had gone to their individual apartments. My grandfather was the eldest son and, as is done out of respect for any family member who dies, the kitchen stoves were not to be lit and food was not to be cooked till the shraddha ceremony was completed.

Having eaten the dinner sent by our relatives, we lingered around the adults, listening to their stories. I used to be terrified of going to sleep by myself in my grandparents' bedroom at the other end of the courtyard for it meant crossing the long, empty corridors with shuttered doors along the shadowy thakur dalan. Each room was vast and had a sitting area with sofas and diwans, a large round marble table and enormous wall mirrors that reflected the light of the hand-cut crystal lamps. On the far end were massive teak cupboards with carved elephant heads and legs shaped like lion paws. The four-poster beds, also made of dark teak, had railings on either side in case you rolled off, and were furnished with bolsters to keep you cosy and protected, and could be accessed by stepping on a stool.

Having changed into my pyjamas, I climbed into bed and crawled under the heavy mosquito netting gingerly to ensure no insect followed me in. Sleeping with my mother and grandmother was a treat: I loved the smell of their starched white saris and their hair oil, the soft pillows, including my baby pillow which travelled with me everywhere and without which I couldn't sleep. My small wood-carved elephant, placed carefully under my pillow, provided me with a sense of undefined protection wherever I went. Our bedtime routine was to have Didibhai tell us a story as she stroked our foreheads, murmuring 'shaat shaat' as she soothed us to sleep.

I loved her stories and I loved the gods, but most of all I loved to dream—of gods and goddesses, demons and ogres, the distant trumpeting of elephants and the roar of the tiger and the clash of metal loud enough to freeze the blood in your veins.

As I lay in bed that night, my head on my pillow with my protective wooden elephant under it, I waited for my mother and grandmother to settle down after what must have been an exhausting day of ceremonies and endless visitors. As I was wondering how to coax a story out of them, I suddenly saw a dismembered hand holding a curved scimitar, with its blade flashing in the light, cut across the mosquito net.

I leapt up with a bloodcurdling scream that bounced off the marble floors and ricocheted off the walls—and woke up the household. My uncle and aunt, the guard and the staff all rushed into the room. Gasping for breath, in between sobs, I gabbled on about what I had seen. I was very sure that I had not imagined it. My grandmother too said that she had seen something. I insisted that every room be opened up and checked. A thorough search followed: cobwebs were brushed away, curtains parted, beds upturned, cupboards flung open as room after room was checked for an intruder. But there was none.

That image continues to be etched in my memory even today. And though it took me years to recognize that this was perhaps my first conscious encounter with a dark energy of some kind, I have never been able to make sense of the horror of that moment. It was not as if my grandfather was murdered or had suffered a violent death that had projected this image. I still wonder if this was a visitation from the past? An image from a previous life? Or my own mind playing out an undefined terror?

2

An Eerie Presence

Tughlaq Road, New Delhi

We moved to Delhi in 1970. Coming from Bombay, my first glimpse of this new city made me feel like I had stepped into a different world, free of traffic and double-decker buses but lacking the expanse of the Arabian Sea and the food vendors of Chowpatty Beach.

Everything was different. The vast bungalows of Lutyens' Delhi replaced Bombay's multi-storeyed homes. INA and Khan Market became our new shopping haunts instead of Colaba Causeway and Sahakari Bhandar. Marine Drive and Flora Fountain gave way to flower-bedecked roundabouts, and the

Hanging Gardens of Malabar Hill to the dewy expanse of Lodhi Garden. Fluffy clouds of bhatura with chole and gulab jamun at Bengali Market replaced mutton frankies and Parsi Dairy kulfi. India Gate, resplendent on Rajpath, with the dome of the Rashtrapati Bhawan framed by the setting sun in the distance, replaced the Gateway of India and the waves crashing upon its steps as boats roiled and rocked to an invisible beat. Those first impressions of Delhi have remained with me and laid the foundation of my continued love affair with this now frenetic city of politics and power, traffic jams and pollution.

This was more than five decades ago, long before terror attacks and assassinations brought in police barricades, barbed wire and Z-class security. The advent of a resurgent India fuelled by a new economic order was yet to be seen: its march towards progress, marked by multiplexes and malls, highways and flyovers, was still invisible. Those were gentler times—of school socials and New Year's Eve parties, Gymkhana Club chicken sandwiches and French fries, reading rooms and libraries.

Our new home, 93 Lodhi Estate, was a Lutyens' style bungalow with a vast lawn. It was fitted with a huge desert cooler, the khus-scented breeze from which would cool the house in summer. I studied at Mount St. Mary's School, situated in the Delhi cantonment area which was about 10 km away; I headed out every morning in the school bus that stopped outside the house. School appeared foreign and I couldn't quite relate to my classmates who had grown up together and formed a bond which was difficult to break through. My abiding memory is of being made to stand by the roadside, waving flags as visiting heads of state drove past our school.

As the 1971 Bangladesh Liberation War approached, we dug trenches in the school field and practised evacuation drills; hunkering down in the pits was part of our routine as there was a growing awareness of a possible attack on India, particularly Delhi, and we were constantly reminded of what our response should be if the sirens went off.

At the time I didn't know that Pa had been posted as the Director of Naval Intelligence and had launched a covert operation to train 1,000 Mukti Bahini cadres made up of soldiers, students and civilians who had grouped together in response to the Pakistani military's crackdown on Bengalis in erstwhile East Pakistan. They would be taught guerrilla tactics and underwater manoeuvres in order to detonate limpet mines on cargo ships, which, when executed, led to the blockade of the Chittagong harbour amongst others, contributing to India's victory in the war.

The grimness of war was alleviated somewhat by the presence of Pluto, our miniature pug. He was our love and life. He had come to us as a puppy, to fill the void left behind by Choppy, our Pomeranian who had passed away. More human than dog, Pluto learnt to wipe his paws when he came indoors, loved having his teeth brushed, jumped straight into bed and cuddled up to us when no one was watching, and kept us entertained in the days when there was no television or mobile phones. He truly was the sweetest dog ever and Dada and I doted on him. When he died at the end of the year, it broke all our hearts. Dada played the 'Last Post' on his bugle, which he had learnt to play at Lawrence School, Lovedale, tears streaming down his face. Life post Pluto's passing seemed unreal and dreamlike. For a long time, I would look back at my childhood as having been divided in two parts: when Pluto was there, a time filled with joy and happiness, and when he had passed, an unhappy dream we somehow lived through.

We moved to London after the 1971 war, where I instantly adopted Fredrick, the school hamster who, we later discovered, was actually Fredrika! On weekends we travelled to strawberry farms, holidayed in a caravan in the Lake District, and drove up to Sterling Castle and Glasgow, where a gigantic dog swallowed our socks and slippers in one gulp. Dada and I wore purple bell-bottoms and sported long hair. I learnt to play the violin, crushed on my French teacher, went swimming at Crystal Palace, bunked school lunches on Thursdays and went to Dulwich village to eat hot dogs and Mars bars and a champagne lolly (all for one pound, which was our weekly pocket money), helped my brother steal dinky cars from the toy shop, watched colour television in the evenings—*The Basil Brush Show*, *Voyage to the Bottom of the Ocean*, *Star Trek* (the original series)—and watched our first musical and sang along to

Jesus Christ
Jesus Christ
Who are you? What have you sacrificed?
Jesus Christ
Jesus Christ
Who are you? What have you sacrificed?
Jesus Christ
Superstar
Do you think you're what they say you are?
Jesus Christ
Superstar
Do you think you're what they say you are?

Dada and I invariably fought when our parents were away socializing in the evenings, and I used to argue endlessly with our eldest cousin Nipu (Tuhin), who was staying with us while studying in London. Once, having tripped up Dada on his roller skates, I sprinted back to the house with him in hot pursuit and slammed the double-glazed glass door in his face. Unable to break his run, he sailed through the glass and ended up on the carpeted hallway, covered in shards, blood oozing from cuts all over his body. It was a heart-stopping moment for both of us as I screamed the house down, wondering if I had killed him and terrified of the consequences once our parents returned. Dada survived the incident, and we went on to play Monopoly and Scrabble and raced on his Scalextric set—and fought till a new day dawned. I brought home my first girlfriend, a Brit of African descent who was twice my size, much to the amusement of my mother and father who were at home; we sat in the garden and played ball with Fredrika even as my girlfriend marvelled at our carpeted foyer and colour television.

A year or so later, in 1973, we headed back to Bombay as Pa, who had assumed he would stay on as Naval Attaché to the High Commission of India in London, received the good news that he had been appointed captain of the INS *Vikrant*, where he had earlier served with the INAS 310 Squadron. Dada and I were admitted to the Cathedral and John Connon School, located in the Fort area. I loved school and excelled in elocution contests—where I once won a first prize with a rendition from Alan Paton's *Cry, the Beloved Country*, having been coached by the legendary Mrs Jeffries. I discovered the delicious kanda keri (raw mango and chopped onions) that was sold outside senior school and got hooked to it! I learnt Hindi and took Sanskrit classes, replete with *aham gachhami*, and went on a school excursion to the Elephanta Caves, holding hands with my girlfriend as the waves crashed upon the ferry. I invariably got into trouble and was often thrown out of class by Vijaya Ghose, the most wonderful class teacher ever, for playing chess under her nose and writing impassioned letters to girls in my class.

I returned to Delhi in 1977 to join my parents, and though I have travelled the world, the city has remained home for me ever since. I moved from my parents' home at 3 Teen Murti Marg to the residence at St. Stephen's College, and after that to a rented barsaati in Sundar Nagar with Pankaj Bajpayee, a college mate, and when he left Delhi, I lived with the Saxenas, my friend Manoj's family, in R.K. Puram where I used to return in the middle of the night after rehearsals and partying. One night, the driver of the three-wheeler I was in, who appeared drunk and was singing lustily into the night, toppled over, resulting in a fractured elbow for me. The guilt-stricken driver righted the vehicle and took me home. When Pinky (Manjari Nigam), Manoj's elder sister, opened the door, she saw my bedraggled state and burst out laughing, an incident she relates even today.

Post university and many a rebellion later, I came back home to 27 Tughlaq Road. By then, Pa had retired as Commander-in-Chief of the Eastern Naval Command and had returned to Delhi as Secretary to the Government of India to head India's nuclear submarine programme at the behest of the then Prime Minister Indira Gandhi, Dr Raja Ramanna and the then Defence Minister R. Venkataraman.

Our new home, a three-acre estate that sat at the intersection of Safdarjung Road, Prithviraj Road and Tughlaq Road, was witness to the riots of 1984. As news spread about Mrs Gandhi's assassination, a turbaned Sikh was dragged off his scooter and burnt at the crossing right outside our house. Appalled by the violence that was engulfing the city even as we returned from paying our respects to Mrs Gandhi at Teen Murti Bhawan where her body lay in state, I rushed off to the Jor Bagh taxi stand to check on the Sikh drivers who used to ferry me daily to office as I hadn't learnt to drive yet and asked them to take shelter in our home till the situation was brought under control.

Puneeta and I had planned to get engaged on 31 October 1984; instead, over the next few days, we heeded the call for help from Kanika Satyanand and an NGO collective, the Nagrik Ekta Manch, to go out to the embattled Sikh communities and offer up whatever aid was possible. Walking through the torched, bloodied, slipper-strewn streets of east Delhi, littered with half-burnt bodies, their fingers clenched in horror and pain, was horrific; the stench of burning flesh and the images from those days would haunt us for a long while. It's sad that many of the perpetrators of the violence were never held accountable for their crimes even to this date.

Puneeta and I had met at Theatre Action Group (TAG); she joined a year or so after me. Her sister, Poonam, was a friend of Sita Raina, an actor and executive member of TAG. Puneeta had just been transferred to Delhi from Bombay, where she had been working with Western Outdoor Advertising, and felt lost without her friends. I had joined TAG while I was studying philosophy at St. Stephen's. Theatre was my passion and much of my college life was spent working in street theatre productions, focusing on social issues such as bride burning, dowry and women's empowerment, as well as protesting society's many ills.

When Dilip Simeon, a legendary professor at Ramjas College, was set upon by goons on the supposed instructions of the principal, civil society organizations came together to protest the brutal beating which had Dilip laid up in hospital for over six months, battling for his life. We demanded that the thugs be arrested and the principal be dismissed. But all this was easier said than done. The principal refused to resign and had a gang of goons come and beat us up. The police, called onto the campus by the principal, arrested us instead of the perpetrators. As the news of our arrest spread, hundreds of students showed up and blocked the police van that was transporting us to the local thana. The cops panicked and decided to release us, but we refused to get off the police van till an FIR was filed against those who had beaten us up, leading to an impasse till they agreed to drop all charges against us and inquire into what had happened.

Standing up to the arbitrariness of those in power has always been second nature for me. It has invariably got me into trouble and I thank my Bengali genes for this. When the then principal of St. Stephen's College, the Rt Reverend Rajpal, brought in new rules for those in residence—including making it mandatory for students to sign in every night, attend morning assembly, and not paper over or cover the windows in our rooms in the residence—I set down a ladder in front of his office with a large satirical poster of a Peeping Tom and went on a hunger strike. What began as a prank during Practical Joke (PJ) Week grew into a movement with residents boycotting meals in the dining hall in support of the call to action. While the principal hated me for questioning his authority, there was little he could do but reluctantly accept some of the demands put before him by our professors.

When Pakistan's President Zia-ul-Haq was invited to the college, his alma mater, we went on a signature campaign, protesting that a dictator shouldn't be allowed into the hallowed corridors of St. Stephen's where freedom fighters like C.F. Andrews, a confidant of Mahatma Gandhi's, had taught—much to the dismay of the principal who was all set to receive a head of state and enjoy his moment of glory.

Given my activist commitments, I barely attended classes and my professors, barring Dr Gupta, the legendary head of our department and a blue-blooded philosopher, had not met me during the first two terms. As the end of the year approached, I sat down to pen a letter to my parents, stating how uncomfortable I was with the idea of being in a place of privilege and that I wished to devote my life to the upliftment of those who had no voice—I was intent on going to work in the villages of Bihar and Uttar Pradesh. Dada, the resident brain of the family who was studying for his master's at Delhi School of Economics, dropped by to check on me and offered up sage advice, saying that while it was wonderful that I wanted to save the world, it was unlikely that I would survive the rigours of village life without air conditioning and the occasional chicken sandwich, and that the only bomb I would be throwing would be out of the window of a limousine. His words struck a chord and I was left wondering how best to redeem the situation. As it happened, Pankaj Bajpayee, a classmate in the philosophy department, was directing a student film with Prof. Vijay 'Tanks' Tankha. They needed an actor and believed I would fit the role opposite Ritu Saigal and Radhey Pratap Singh in a brain-vs-brawn love triangle.

Tanks sent me a note saying should I wish to sit for my final exams, I would need to sort out my attendance and that if I acted in their movie, he would be happy to take additional classes to help make up my attendance and cover the prescribed course work. It was an offer I couldn't resist. Off I went to shoot, which was great fun; I bonded instantly with Professors Vohra and Tankha, and at the end of a long day's shoot we would gorge on mince and scrambled eggs at the college café, or bun samosa at Rohtas's dhaba, where they would tutor us on the fundamentals of Plato and Socrates, logic and Indian philosophy, all of which was fascinating.

The exams rolled in and somewhat magically, I topped the university in the first year, which I put down in equal parts to the special classes held by our professors and my bad handwriting that the examiner had probably not been able to decipher.

In 1980, I was cast as Peter in *The Diary of Anne Frank*, directed by Abha Sood at Lady Shri Ram College. Soon after, Tanks suggested that I audition for TAG as they were casting for a new production. Off I went with Madhav Dar, who had set up the Amateur Theatre Society in college which had got us into a lot of trouble and had consequently got him expelled from the residence, and we were cast as the Venticelli in Peter Shaffer's *Amadeus*. It was a grand production starring Siddharth 'Babu' Basu in the lead role of Mozart and Lillete Dubey as Constance, his wife, with Barry John himself playing Salieri.

Once he learned his lines, Barry was brilliant as only he could be. The artistic director of TAG, he was known for his avant-garde as well as opulent scenography, and for attracting the best talent in the city, culled from St. Stephen's, Miranda House and Lady Shri Ram College. Abha Sood Adams, Amit Bhatia, Asha Kochar, Bharat Kapoor, Khalid Tyabji, Laila Tyabji, Lillete Dubey, Lushin Dubey, Mohit Satyanand, Mira Nair, Pamela Rooks, Ravi and Rajeev Dubey, Rohit Khosla, Radhika Singh, Sanjeev Ahluwalia, Sita Raina and Vidyun Singh were some of the many luminaries who came through the doors of TAG. Later, Divya Seth, Deepika Deshpande, Manoj Bajpayee, Lynne Fernandez, Rituraj Singh, Shah Rukh Khan, Viveka Kumari, Benny Thomas, Ranganathan, Gayathri Vishwanathan, Revathy and Venkat joined the group as active members with daily workshops and rehearsals.

TAG was a place of intense passion and numerous romances blossomed across the ages through workshops and productions, resulting in marriages between Lillete and Ravi Dubey, Vidyun Singh and Sanjeev Singh Ahluwalia (Ahlu), Viveka Kumari and Cecil Qadir, Lushin and Pradeep Dubey, Mohit Satyanand and Premila Nazareth among others.

Puneeta, when she joined TAG, found me insufferable, but in the best Mills & Boon fashion, the perception thankfully didn't last and we soon became inseparable, partying night after night, much to the chagrin of her father. When she was stricken by chickenpox, I used to read up the sports pages to ingratiate myself with her dad and head off to her house every day to keep her company. At some point, Puneeta decided that I had to make a commitment to her and gave me an ultimatum which resulted in us deciding to get engaged at the New Delhi Kali Bari where we exchanged vows; a year and a half later, we were formally married.

Theatre continued to be my life and passion. I spent my days doing production work at Barry's barsaati in Jungpura and evenings rehearsing at the Blind School—then a quick change and it was party time! Theatre workshops and rehearsals knitted us—Lynne, Viveka, Puneeta and me—into a small self-obsessed community, and in those post-graduation days we couldn't get enough of each other. We used to pick up Puneeta and then set off for Viveka's house in Vasant Vihar where Aunty Harshad (Kumari), Ba Saheba, the erstwhile princess of Jamnagar, hosted an open house with a constant supply of food and drinks: Gujarati theplas with a garlic and coriander chutney, an array of achars and sweetmeats, dals, fish, my favourite Sontreli raan and so much more. When not at Viveka's, you could find us at Lynne's home on Hill View Drive in Vasant Vihar, where Aunty June rustled up the most fabulous kathi rolls and mutton chops which we couldn't get enough of. Or we would head to the Raos' Padmini Enclave home where Mona and Seema threw the most booze-fuelled dance parties with delicious south Indian fare and great music. There were late night dashes to Pindi or Havemore on Pandara Road for kebabs and brain curry, butter chicken and rara meat. On special occasions, mostly funded by Puneeta, the only earning member in our theatre tribe, we ended up at the Taj's Machan coffee shop for its hot chocolate fudge and club sandwiches, post which, somewhat wasted, we would crawl back home to bed.

My father often asked Puneeta: 'And how should I introduce my younger son? My elder son is a nuclear economist and physicist; what should I say of Sanjoy?', and my father-in-law, in the run-up to our wedding, had queried me on what I did for a living. I told him I worked in theatre and paid myself Rs 1,000 a month towards expenses. On being asked how that would help in supporting his daughter, I replied that his daughter was the manager of Western Outdoor Advertising and would be supporting us. Certainly not a convincing argument to make to the father of your future bride, and that ultimately led me to join Bobby and Varsha Bedi in their newly formed TV company, B.V. Videographics, and direct *Telefun*, the first game show for India's national broadcaster, Doordarshan.

Our Tughlaq Road house had a sweeping driveway with separate entry and exit gates, an outhouse which doubled as Pa's home office and extensive lawns that stretched out at the back. Recessed at the far end were the garages and staff quarters to accommodate the maali, the dhobi, the cook Nirmala and her son Bechu, and other household staff.

Enormous master bedrooms, with two attached bathrooms, flanked the drawing room. In earlier times, they had served the burra sahib and his memsahib, each tended to separately by their personal staff. (In retrospect, these were excellent arrangements that, I suspect, led to far less acrimony between couples than what we experience these days with shared bathroom facilities and differing standards of order and hygiene.)

The family room had a false ceiling and a working air conditioner and TV; it doubled as my bedroom at night. The back veranda had long been converted into a dining area from where you could step out onto the lawns—where peacocks roamed, squirrels scampered and the mango and jamun trees cast a magical spell in the winter mist.

At the end of the driveway, secluded by tall bushes and trees, Riaz bhai built sets for TAG's theatre productions, designed by Barry John. The revolving set of *Noises Off*, which cost an arm and a leg, *A Map of the World*, *Metamorphosis* and *Rough Crossing* were constructed there, as were the sets for the madly eccentric game show *Telefun*, that needed outlandish props which were transported to different cities where we video-recorded the episodes.

I have always dreamt in 70 mm, fuelled in part by the day's events and peppered with images from whatever book I am reading, or a film that we might have seen recently. A poor sleeper at the best of times, music is usually the only way for me to calm down. Over the years, Pink Floyd, Carly Simon, Elvis Presley, the Beatles, the Eagles, Supertramp, Beethoven, Mozart, Simon and Garfunkel, Queen, Bon Jovi, Sting, Bade Ghulam Ali Khan, Jagjit and Chitra Singh, ABBA and Boney M have all found space in my ever-expanding audio collection. At the time, turntables and LP record players had been consigned to history. We had a brand-new cassette player along with a portable three-in-one contraption with a radio, TV and cassette player that had an automatic stop function. It was the sound of this stop button clicking back into place that may have been the cause of my nightmares.

Many a night, I was jolted awake with the sense of an ominous presence looming above me, right next to my bed. I would struggle to break free, my mouth stretching wide open in a scream that remained stuck in my throat even as a dark ginormous energy filled the room, sucking out the oxygen from my lungs. Though I tried screaming for help, I remained paralysed, my hair standing on end, sweat beading my forehead as I lay helpless, consumed by the presence of this spirit, which stared at me unmoving, its blood-red eyes awash with anger. Fighting off my sleep paralysis, I would scramble to turn on the lights and the presence would fade away. I would pad through the house which was quiet, air coolers humming in the distance, the guard on his duty round and my parents fast asleep. I would try and calm myself down by drinking cold water, switching on as many lights as possible and checking all the rooms and the bathrooms before reluctantly getting back into bed.

These visitations happened at regular intervals over many months and it was some years later, when I was jolted awake during a similar episode, that I wondered if it was the cassette player making the sound of the click as the automatic switch turned the system off, that triggered my deep-seated fear.

3

The Tantrics

Khajuraho

The wind rustled through the leaves of the tall ashoka trees on the banks of the Shivsagar Lake, which shimmered like molten gold in the late afternoon sun. Khajuraho's western group of temples, built a millennium ago, had witnessed a thousand years of wars and conquests, celebrations and destructions. Over time, they had been submerged under an ever-spreading camouflage of creepers, undergrowth, trees and shrubs that took sustenance from the water bodies all around.

Nature, which forms the basis of all worship, had reclaimed ground, a final conquest against man who, spurred on by greed and ego, possession and power, practised destruction as the path to glory, forgetting that long before we walked the earth, nature alone had prevailed, and it would continue to do so long after we bombed ourselves to extinction.

In 1838, British army captain T.S. Burt hacked his way through the dense jungle and was astounded by the scale and grandeur of the monumental structures he discovered. They were covered with tantric friezes and beautifully sculpted men and women revelling in various stages of shringar and sexual pleasure. Majestic processions of elephants and horses were celebrated in stone, representative of a thriving economic community—Kharjuravahaka. This was a place where kings and queens and influential merchants would come to pay obeisance, seek favours and ask for blessings and forgiveness; they would pray for victory against their enemies, or for good health, love and material success.

Built between the ninth and twelfth centuries by the Chandela dynasty, the Khajuraho temples are known for their Nagara style of architecture—tall, curved towers or shikharas rising from the sanctum sanctorum. The estimated eighty-five temples in the western, eastern and southern groups, of which only twenty-five survive today, were Hindu or Jain in nature.

The western group of temples is the most impressive and consists of the imposing Kandariya Mahadeva Temple, where every Shivratri, processions and rituals are still staged to pay homage to and celebrate Lord Shiva and his union with his consort, Shakti. The Lakshmana Temple is devoted to Lord Vishnu, as is the Varaha Temple which features a monolithic image of the boar incarnation of Vishnu, who burrows into the underworld to rescue Bhairavi–Mother Earth–who was kidnapped and taken to the bottom of the cosmic ocean by the demon king Hiranyaksha, causing chaos and destruction on earth.

The head priests or tantrics of this fabled temple town were among the most powerful people in the Chandela courts. They were regarded as the gatekeepers to the gods they had inherited, and to the kings and queens they served; they weighed the favours bestowed upon them, using powerful mantras to bless those who sought them or destroy those whom they considered as threats to their power and existence.

The Chausath Yogini complex, built in the late ninth century, is one of the oldest structures in the temple town. Dedicated to the sixty-four yoginis, the temple represents different aspects of the divine feminine and is set in a circular plan which is rare in Hindu temple architecture.

In 1999, to commemorate the thousandth anniversary of these temples, which were completed by 999 CE, and also to mark the millennium, Pramila and Kanti Poddar, owners of the hotel Taj Khajuraho, in conjunction with the Archaeological Survey of India (ASI), the Madhya Pradesh state government and the Confederation of Indian Industry (CII), had invited the President of India to visit the temple town. Teamwork, our company, had been commissioned by Ajay Shankar, the then director general of the ASI, to produce a cultural extravaganza to mark the occasion.

We visited Khajuraho a number of times in preparation for this major event, became well versed with the history and architectural tradition of the temple complex, and learnt about the aspects of tantric worship that were evident from the sculptures and yantras carved in stone. Each evening, after a gruelling day spent figuring out how best to fill up the Shiv Kund with water in a sustainable manner using the existing canals so that it wouldn't dry up in the future, or working with the district collector and the commissioner to clean up the town in anticipation of the visit, or bringing on board local craftspeople, hotels and village folk, and coordinating with the architects from the Indian National Trust for Art and Cultural Heritage who had been tasked with creating the signage and effective lighting of the complexes, we would return to the newly opened Lalit Hotel to ideate and resolve the challenges ahead.

The show envisaged a magnificent procession, including a gigantic float—designed by master puppeteer

Dadi Pudumjee in the form of the sun—with hundreds of musicians and performers, that would make its way over the water body, and conclude with pyrotechnics and the release of a thousand paper lanterns into the night sky to mark the millennium. The challenges of creating this spectacular production on the Shiv Kund were considerable. The town itself was a conglomeration of seven villages and had no infrastructure or facilities apart from the hotels and what they offered in terms of comfort and food. From the lighting and sound systems to the complexities of pyrotechnics, every prop had to be sourced or created and then transported into the town over pockmarked roads. We had requested the army to build us a raft that would be stable and easy to steer and also capable of carrying the many musicians and performers as it was to be the centrepiece of the procession across the Shiv Kund. Much of this was made possible through the personal intervention of the then chief minister of Madhya Pradesh, Digvijay Singh, who understood the urgency of decision-making and wanted to cut through the red tape that would have otherwise had us running from pillar to post, begging bowl in hand, to get anything done. He regularly presided over meetings, ensuring that we had all possible support from the local administration in executing our vision and dealing with the minutiae of protocol surrounding a presidential visit.

One evening, huddled together in my suite at the Lalit, we were deeply engrossed in working through the show's flow which needed precise timing and multiple rehearsals with different departments and performers to ensure a flawless execution. The idea was to have the float approach the presidential platform with the music reaching a crescendo and fireworks that would light up the sky, and as these died out, the thousand paper lanterns would be lit and released into the night.

Exhausted by the never-ending meetings, Puneeta had crawled into bed, covered herself with a white linen bedsheet and fallen fast asleep, oblivious to our ongoing discussions. I have always marvelled at her ability to fall into deep sleep regardless of the place, or the noise or light around her. Something that's almost impossible for me to do.

Our production crew, including Sharupa, Manika, Deepali, Deepika, Vandana, Yamini and Dilip, were sitting in a circle at the foot of the bed, some leaning against it or propped up on bolsters while others were seated on chairs. From where I was sitting, I could see Puneeta asleep on the bed. Suddenly, the sheet that she had covered herself with appeared to levitate, with her body convulsing from head to toe. I scrambled up and dashed to her, calling out her name and trying to wake her up, but to no avail. Her body and the sheet undulated like windswept waves in a lake till the convulsions subsided. She woke up, oblivious to what had happened, and was perturbed to see us peering down at her with a collective look of horror on our faces.

We recounted the incident to her and asked her what she had experienced. She said she hadn't felt anything at all and was totally unaware of what had transpired. I held on to Puneeta, seeking comfort and reassurance that all was well, while the others, completely spooked, fled from the suite and headed to their own rooms.

The commemoration was magnificent, and the visit of President K.R. Narayanan was a success; the programme garnered a great deal of attention for Khajuraho and briefly contributed to its economy. On our return to Delhi, still puzzled as to what exactly had occurred that night, we went to the Karmic Research Centre (KRC) and consulted Gurudev, our ascended master.

Gurudev was ever calm and had a deep understanding of the most complex situations. He suggested that Puneeta undertake a past life regression session. Through a guided meditation, he took her back many lifetimes to a thousand years ago to Khajuraho, where she had apparently been a tantric priestess. I was a powerful tantric head priest who had misused my position and powers for self-aggrandizement, and, filled with greed and ego, had sought sexual fulfilment.

Puneeta was a priestess with siddhis (or powers) bestowed upon her through tapasya—practising extreme self-discipline, meditation and penance to purify the mind, body and soul in order to achieve spiritual growth and self-realization. She had come to Khajuraho to challenge me, but it seems she was unsuccessful, and my powers and spells had pushed her over the brink into insanity. The regression got more complicated as friends from this lifetime were also present then, playing key roles as aides, procurers and deputies to the head tantric, and they were all impacted by the tragedy that unfolded against the backdrop of Khajuraho.

A thousand years later, it appears we had all chosen to be reborn together in this present lifetime to work through our entangled karma and find ways to forgive and heal. We still don't quite know what happened that night and what possessed Puneeta, but the image of her undulating body has stayed vividly in my mind.

4

There Will Be Blood

Safdarjung Enclave, New Delhi

A shriek rent the air, wrenching us out of peaceful slumber. Disoriented, we sat up and saw our two-year-old son Avik staring out into the darkness, panic in his eyes, mumbling, 'Woh aa rahi hain (She is coming).'

The pillow and the bedsheet were bloody, streaks of red slashed across the white sheet, glowing as only blood can in the pale moonlight filtering in through the windows. Outside, a peepul tree stood sentinel to the lost souls who had found purchase on its dark brooding branches.

Safdarjung Enclave in south Delhi was built in the 1960s on what used to be the burial grounds for the many dynasties that had once ruled Delhi. As the construction workers began work, they didn't quite grasp that they were trampling upon souls laid to rest over centuries, some casualties of court intrigues and power struggles or petty brawls, others put to death on the whims and fancies of their masters, cut down by daggers or swords. The ghouls, forced to surrender their earthly resting ground to new tenements, had nowhere to go and no recourse but to seek refuge in the recesses of the peepul tree. There they sat, peering in through the windows of the houses that had displaced them, longing to be part of family gatherings, to feast at tables laden with kebabs and sweetmeats, to run through dimly lit corridors with an exuberance they had once possessed, and to experience life itself! Occasionally, they would haunt Puneeta's office, located above us on the third floor, and frighten her colleagues out of their wits.

This wasn't the first haunting in our new home in Safdarjung Enclave, which we had moved into in the summer of 1988. Lenny and Mahesh, Puneeta's colleagues who worked in her office, would encounter headless soldiers resting behind doors, or souls shackled in chains pacing the terrace, looking in on the flurry of activity that characterizes any film company. Did they want to audition, join a conversation, or sip some chai? Or were they looking for revenge against those who had imprisoned them, decapitated them and then left them to rot?

I have been blessed with acute hearing, picking up frequencies and sounds from a distance, broken bits of conversations floating through doors, urgent endearments and angry exchanges beyond brick walls. Lying awake as insomniacs often do, I could tune in to the whispering of anguished souls, each demanding to be heard, their issues addressed. It was initially fascinating—a window to another dimension! Conversing with these 'others' while the air conditioner hummed quietly, filling the room with sleep, Puneeta's soft grunts punctuated by the urgent tick-tock of the bedside clock winding its way to a new dawn—was entertaining till it became overwhelming. As the corners of the room overflowed with vague shapes hugging the walls, afraid of stepping out into the faint light in case it made them disappear before they could seek redressal, 'ghosts of the past arise and come forth' seemed to be the rallying call. Often, I would sit up in anger at the intrusion and tell them all to bugger off and let me sleep, but to little avail. They wailed, they wept, they pleaded, they threatened until I had heard each one of them. I can't quite recall what was said: some were entreaties seeking redressal, others were pleas for messages to be passed on, and most were nothing more than the indistinguishable mumblings of the broken-hearted!

As the first light filtered tenuously through the leaves of the peepul tree and the room emptied out, I would fall into a deep sleep, oblivious to the stirrings of the family, the kids being readied for school, the kitchen coming to life, Tugu (Tughlaq, our hybrid labrador–dachshund, named after our former residence on Tughlaq Road) being taken out for his constitutional walk. Tugu was fiercely loyal to the kids, having arrived when our first-born son, Aditya, was six months old (Avik followed three and a half years later); he would snap at anyone who came near the boys and, I suspect, guarded them from otherworldly beings as well.

Morning showers were an event in themselves. As the hot water steamed up the bathroom and fogged the mirror, the imprint of two skeletal hands would appear on it. Curious as to why this happened only when I took a bath, Puneeta asked Gurudev for an explanation. He told her that these were imprints of our guides who were there to protect us from malevolent forces and offer help when needed. Gurudev explained that we are born with guides or guardian angels who are tasked with helping us navigate our life and steer through our worldly chores. These are the voices we hear if we are open to them; the 'instinct' that arises suddenly, warning us of danger, to look back or step aside, or tilt our head just in the nick of time, or take a decision which defies logic but later turns out to be to our benefit. Most of us have little awareness of our destiny or our life goals when we are born, let alone of the existence of our guides. More often than not, we ignore these messages, allowing them to get lost in the turmoil of our daily lives and in the pursuit of a livelihood. He added that we are born in soul clusters, with attachments to each other from our past lives, returning to pay back a debt or to experience another life together, where relationships and sexes are interchangeable between parents and siblings, lovers and enemies, soulmates and friends.

Avik, our younger son, came into our lives at a difficult time. Puneeta and I were struggling to keep it together. Caught up in a slew of ongoing TV productions which were followed by a whirlwind of socializing and parties every evening, I felt tied down by familial and parental responsibilities. Puneeta, who was busy with her own productions, including her popular talk show *Shakti*, preferred to spend time with Aditya at the end of a long day. We seemed to be pulling in different directions and, unknown to me, she had been contemplating finding her own way ahead.

We were in Calcutta for the wedding of Apu (Arup), our universally loved first cousin, who was the closest to Dada. Enroute to the wedding, as we were passing through Asansol, my mother began to feel very uncomfortable and complained of angina and a tightening in her chest. We made a detour to the hospital where they examined her, treated her for the chest pain and then discharged her as they didn't have a heart specialist on duty. We continued to the wedding and returned home to Lansdowne Road two days later.

My mother, very much the ginni-ma (boss of the household), was barking out instructions to her two daughters-in-law from her bed, telling them which piece of jewellery should be worn to match with which sari, when she suddenly began convulsing. We called the doctors, who said she was in the throes of a major heart attack, rushed her to the Army hospital and admitted her to the CCU. The attack, the result of major blockages in her arteries, compromised a third of her heart muscles and necessitated open-heart surgery some years later.

Meanwhile, Puneeta, unused to the never-ending string of wedding festivities that began with fried fish and sweets in the morning and ended with mangsho and chingri maach (meat and prawns) at night, began feeling unwell and couldn't keep her food down. Convinced that she had contracted jaundice or had food poisoning, we got her blood tests done on our return to Delhi.

It was Pa who picked up the test report from Dr Dang's. He came home with a twinkle in his eyes and gave us the news that Puneeta was expecting. We were both stunned as that wasn't quite what *we* were expecting—yet, if it hadn't been for these glad tidings and the arrival of an enlightened being in our midst, Puneeta and I may have separated.

From Avik's very arrival, we realized that raising him was going to be an exceptional experience. His frequent shrieks that scrambled our souls in the middle of the night made us sit bolt upright, dread and sweat pouring down our bodies. Then there was the blood. These were no ordinary episodes of a child crying, and the bleeding was inexplicable. We consulted our paediatrician, Dr Priti Pargal, for solutions to the nightly bloodletting. She put it down to a nosebleed and prescribed a treatment plan, but the bleeding refused to stop.

We were frantic parents in search of answers, wondering if this was something more serious—an intestinal issue perhaps? Or blood gushing from an ulcer in his mouth? We were willing to try anything to address the problem. Then, one day, a college mate, Madhav Dar, dropped in.

Madhav was a year senior to me in college, as were most of my friends: Sam (Samir Sahu), Fats (Manoj Saxena), Kev (Kevyn David), Rana (Aditya), WPS (Wahi Pal Singh Sidhu) and the very eccentric Rajiv Jha, who appeared at my first freshers' ragging session with a tie around his neck and said, 'I was trying to hang myself but this tie is too short!'

Madhav loved theatre. It was he who proposed that we set up the Amateur Theatre Society while we were in St. Stephen's, much to the chagrin of the college authorities who were hell-bent on throwing us out. He was also smitten by the fairest of them all, Gunjan Ralhan, who was studying history and who had most men in St. Stephen's and Hindu College swooning over her. Madhav was particularly taken by her ankles and was keen that I cast her in Peter Shaffer's *Equus*, which I went on to direct with him in the lead role. The play ran to full houses in Shri Ram Centre but almost bankrupted us all. Rags (Sujata Raghavan), my schoolmate, was the head of production and had valiantly raised the resources to stage the play; she was aghast to find that we had eaten and drunk our way through the sponsorship money.

Post our graduation, Madhav had left for New York to pursue his master's degree at Stony Brook and upon returning, he joined Jawaharlal Nehru University to complete his doctorate where he met Nirupama, his to-be wife.

A Kashmiri who had lived in Calcutta for several years, Madhav was steeped in the occult and was a Shiv bhakt. On hearing what had been happening, he concluded that Avik was possibly an 'old soul' and dear to the Goddess Kali who wanted him back. According to him, it was she who manifested herself in Avik's dreams at night, causing him to shout, 'Woh aa rahi hain!' Madhav gave Puneeta a mantra and suggested that she recite it each day to appease the goddess, and said that this would stop the bleeding. Desperate for a solution, Puneeta recited the prayer daily and over the next few weeks, the bleeding and Avik's nightmares did stop.

The only remnant of that spine-chilling period in our lives is Avik's continued phobia of ketchup, and of anything that even remotely looks like blood.

5

'Woh Gandi Wali Hain'

Narkanda

Screaming, Pushpa didi ran out of the room, her hair on fire, her hands frantically slapping her head, panicked and crazed by what had happened. Fear pierced our martini-infused haze and we hastily threw a blanket around her and doused the sparks on her singed eyebrows. The smell of burnt hair spread through the room. The kids huddled together, terrified, looking desperately to us for a sense of calm and normalcy.

Nestled in the middle Himalayas is the sleepy town of Narkanda; it comes alive each winter as a skiing destination, and in summer, becomes a refuge for tourists from the plains in search of cool days and nostalgic evenings, accompanied by rum and whiskey, bonfires and music. As you drive through Shimla, past Wildflower Hall and Kufri, the conifer and oak trees mingle with the maple and poplar which cover the steep slopes. Across the next range of valleys are the magnificent white peaks of the Greater Himalayan Range, glistening in the sunlight. Further down the terraced hills, apple orchards and idyllic village homes built with local wood and stone mark every bend of the road. Once you turn the last corner of the ridge, the valley falls away and you find yourself driving past the local temple with its presiding deity now located in the middle of the road, with the higgledy-piggledy bazaar on either side—a brush stroke of vermillion, red bangles and flowers—taking you back a hundred years; tea shops and local dhabas serve up hot jalebis, crisp samosas stuffed with spicy potatoes, and thick, over-sweet milky tea.

Cheap lodgings dot the hillside, hostelries built in stark contrast to the beauty of the surroundings, cut into the mountainside, ugly monstrosities painted in hues of pink, blue and green, sporting leaky taps, gnawed footpaths, cracked glass windows and sludge-covered roofs, and heaps of garbage spilling out onto the street. These deep gashes of modernity stood out against the brilliance of the white velvety mountain peaks, washed in hues of orange, pink and purple from the setting sun.

It was a long Republic Day weekend in 1993 and Narkanda was covered in snow, up to three feet deep in places, sparkling in the headlights of our cars as we drove along, leaving the town behind for the only decent accommodation to be found—a beautiful glass-fronted government guest house on top of the far ridge that Tarun (Tejpal) had booked in advance through his journalist contacts.

Mohit, Sujata, Tarun, Geetan, Puneeta and I, and the kids Tiya, Cara, Aditya and Avik, and Pushpa didi had journeyed up, carrying a mountain of food with us as usual, dreading the possibility of having to suffer parathas fried in reheated oil—the standard fare at remote government circuit houses. So, a variety of cheeses, hams, tinned spam, cocktail sausages, baked beans, sardines in tomato sauce and anchovies in oil, dark chocolates, red wine and whiskey by the gallon, Maggi noodles for the kids, and numerous packets of Uncle Chipps and Crax had travelled up with us—enough to feed the entire village if need be!

A winter storm broke as we drove past Narkanda, carpeting the mountainside in bridal white. In a little while, it had cut off the guest house from the town and buried our cars under many feet of snow. We sat out the days playing cards, chatting, reading and drinking, solving the myriad problems of the world and being entertained by our kids. Avik, two and a half years old, had taken to bed the minute we had got there and refused to emerge. Each time we tried to coax him out from under the razai, he mumbled, 'Woh gandi wali hain (She is the evil one),' and dove right back into the bed, with only his eyes peeping out from beneath a red woollen monkey cap.

We had travelled to Narkanda in the past as well, making regular treks through the neighbouring villages where Puneeta and Bete (Sanjeev Saith, photographer, flautist and a few years senior to me in college) were involved in an audio-visual project for UNICEF. We had stayed in a charming village, sharing the villagers' fresh ghee, dal, jungli murgi curry, homemade apple chutney, gur and roti. Each morning, while Puneeta and Bete set out to shoot, I settled down on the wood-carved balcony overlooking the peaks, chatted with the locals, swapped stories and entertained the village kids. As dusk fell, we gathered around an angeethi set in the middle of the room and sang Pahari songs peppered with popular Bollywood tunes. It was idyllic. As we walked up and down the mountainside, we became familiar with the terraced fields and mountain springs, the narrow paths meandering down the valley, lined with wildflowers and bushes with succulent berries, and felt protected by the benign energies all around us. We never encountered anything remotely disruptive, let alone sinister or dark.

This time, though, it was different. The snowstorm lasted two days. On the third day, the dark grey brooding skies gave way to sparkling sunshine that reflected off the vanilla-white ground. The kids played all day in the mounds of snow while we invented brandy golas, a fistful of snow compacted in the palm of our hands to make ice lollies with a generous pour of brandy, which you sucked on. Fortified by whiskey, vodka and wine, we spent hours playing Scrabble and Monopoly or sitting around the fire and chatting. Eventually, as our cache of food dwindled and the last of our Gorgonzola and pepperoni disappeared, we decided to walk to town and see if anyone would help dig our cars out and clear a path for us to leave. We were informed that it would take a few days to commandeer the local JCB which had broken down. The spare part would have to be brought from Rampur, the district headquarters located 60 km away in the next valley, and that would only be possible once the main highway reopened and buses began to ply again. We had no option but to wait it out.

One morning, the kids, happy to be out in the sun, attempted to build a snowman while the adults shaped our now daily ration of brandy golas. Hari, an old acquaintance from the village below, came to greet us and invited us home for apples and chai. We picked our way carefully down the icy slopes, guided expertly by our host who was used to navigating these paths through rain and snow in worn-out sandals, rarely missing a step even when inebriated. We city folks, on the other hand, found it difficult going with our cool Keds, sliding and slithering our way down the steep path to his home with spectacular views of the valley and the mountain peaks.

It was great to meet with Hari and his family and catch up on local gossip. Sitting on his familiar balcony with the winter sun warming us, sipping on chai and looking out at the valley, I spotted what appeared to be a temple built of stone, standing out in stark contrast against the snow, on top of the next mountain peak across the valley. In all our years of visiting Narkanda, none of us had ever noticed that temple before. On enquiring what it was, we were told that it was a local devi shrine, where a form of Goddess Kali was worshipped; it was a place where sacrifices had been offered up in the past. Taken aback, Puneeta and I looked at each other, the same question on both our minds—could this be the 'gandi wali' that Avik had referred to? The villagers were evasive about the antecedents of the temple or the sacrifices conducted there, but spoke instead of the annual fair held at an auspicious time.

When it was time to leave, we hugged our hosts, bade them goodbye and headed back to find the kids still playing in the snow. Pushpa didi, the kids' nanny who had been with us since Aditya was one, was standing guard over Avik who had finally emerged for the first time that week. Settling in for an evening of deep-fried parathas, chicken curry, vodka and whiskey, we marvelled at the number of times Puneeta and I had visited the village without ever laying eyes on the temple.

The kids used to sit in a large glass-encased room which had an iron stove fed with logs to heat the room, keeping them warm and toasty. That night, we were headed upstairs after dinner when we heard bloodcurdling screams and saw Pushpa didi come flying out of the glass room, her hair on fire, running through the corridor in panic, trying to escape the flames which seemed to have engulfed her head.

It turned out that she had opened the door of the stove to add fresh logs and had splashed kerosene from a plastic bottle to give life to the fire. This caused a sudden blast as the flames blazed through the narrow opening, singeing her eyebrows and setting her hair and clothes on fire. The kids looked shocked, and Tiya and Adi ran after her as we threw a blanket over her head which was still sparking, with her hair ends glowing like fireflies. It took us a while to calm her and the kids down before heading off to bed.

The next morning, the JCB, having been repaired, dug out our cars and cleared a path down to the highway through the village. We packed our bags and drove to the main road, peering into the rear-view mirror to catch a glimpse of the 'gandi wali' temple. At Narkanda village, we stopped to pay our respects to the local deity who, our son confirmed, was an 'acchhi wali' (good) goddess.

We drove on and as we turned the corner, the village disappeared behind us. Avik, who hadn't said a word except for 'Woh gandi wali hain' for the past few days, suddenly sprang back to life and was his usual boisterous self all the way down the mountain. How he intuited that there were two separate deities in the region—one who was benign, and another who needed to be propitiated with sacrifices—remains a mystery to this day.

6

Possessed

Rishikesh

I flew off the seat of the bus, breaking free from the five pairs of strong arms holding me down. I seemed to possess demonic energy combined with a sly and devious intent. Each time I felt their hold on me slacken—I broke free, my body arching into the air, lifting off the seat and convulsing wildly. The bus driver, terrified, kept saying, 'Bhoot chadh gaya (He is possessed)!'

Each year as the monsoon surge ebbs and the turbulent waters of the Bhagirathi carve out a new path, fresh sandy embankments are formed. Yousuf and Ganeve—the co-founders of Himalayan River

Runners, among the first professionally run white-water-rafting camps upstream of Rishikesh—set up their base camp on a stretch of the Bhagirathi, 14 km upstream from Rishikesh, for the duration of the season (October through April). Their team navigates new routes around the boulders and the silt carried down from the Himalayas that generate the rapids that visitors experience—Three Blind Mice, the Rollercoaster and, the most terrifying of them all, the Wall, formed by a massive boulder where the river turns into a whirling vortex which you can free yourself from only by rowing furiously in unison: if misjudged, it can result in the crew flying off the raft as it invariably flips over.

We enjoyed our annual pilgrimage to the camp with our kids and friends. Living in tents on the sandy banks of the Ganga, sitting around a roaring fire whose fiery forked tongues reached out to lick the diamond-studded indigo sky, gazing at the Big Dipper, listening to the river cascade by, and swapping stories and life experiences with guests was a way of life. A five-and-a-half-hour drive from Delhi, this was always a much-needed break from the city. Filled with adventure and excitement, even if you had to survive the potty tent, it was a break that we could afford and loved to take as often as possible.

On one such visit, as we sat around the dying embers of a bonfire, counting the shooting stars and the passing satellites, we heard the roar of a tiger and the dying gasps of a wild boar at the end of what must have been a successful hunt in the jungle across from us. In the stillness of the wild, the sound travelled and resonated crystal clear, and it seemed as though the river was the only thing separating us from the tiger. We were scanning the undergrowth and the trees with our torches, the light from which reflected off the silver birch like fireflies rising into the night sky, when suddenly Himangshu Dhanda—a documentary film-maker who co-produced with Rajiv Mehrotra and who had recently given up his status as a confirmed bachelor to marry the wonderful Shalini Jain of Jain Studios—picked up what he thought was the glint of the tiger's eyes swimming towards us. He leapt off his chair in a 'Beam me up, Scottie' moment straight out of *Star Trek* and screamed for Yousuf. The camp jolted awake, and we scampered down to the beach, torches scanning the inky blue river, which revealed nothing. Suddenly, there was a glint and then the clouds plunged us into darkness. It was an Uncle Chipps packet, its foil reflecting the torchlight. So much for a tiger in the wild!

Having teased Dhanda mercilessly about his unexpected athletic prowess, we packed up for the night, crawling into our tents, dusting off the sand and snuggling into our sleeping bags, soothed to sleep by the sound of the river and the occasional screech of a night owl.

The year was 1995. I had been on the road for six months of non-stop travel which had taken a toll on all of us involved in creating what became India's very first television awards, sponsored by Onida TV. Today, the company is remembered for its breakthrough advertising featuring the devil and the tagline, 'Neighbour's envy. Owner's pride.' The award itself, sculpted in metal, was designed as an actor holding his dismembered head in his hands as an offering to the gods. The symbolism escaped us at the time, but it would come back to haunt us and Onida in more ways than one. The awards were meant to cut across all genres and languages, encompassing shows and films from the north and the south, east and west. Endless trips were made to brief TV companies, show producers and directors, and the selection committee members tasked with nominating up to five shows in each category. These, in turn, were to be viewed and scored by an eminent jury and by an academy whose members were well-known faces from the emerging television industry.

The mammoth effort, championed by Sonu Mirchandani, Onida's co-owner, and Giraj Sharma, the company's brilliant marketing head, had been conceived as a tribute to India's entertainment sector, and it kept growing in vision, budget and size. In the early 1990s, the economy had opened up under the then Prime Minister Narasimha Rao and Finance Minister

Manmohan Singh. Together, they had unlocked India's potential, introduced sweeping changes in the way the country looked at business, and were focused on lifting millions out of poverty. TV channels sprouted all around, driven by advertising and new products, with ZEE, EL, DD, BITV, YES, Star, Sony, Sun and Eenadu vying for eyeballs, TRPs and ad revenue, carving up territories in their mission to capture minds, hearts and the all-important TV remote.

Teamwork Films had been part of this TV content boom along with Siddharth and Rosa Basu, Raghav Bahl, Rajat Sharma, Anu Malhotra, Kishwar Ahluwalia, the Alvas' Miditech and the legendary Prannoy and Radhika Roy, pioneers of NDTV. From 1989 to 1995, we produced over fifteen daily and weekly soap operas, game, food and talk shows, and entertainment and satire programmes. We were the new kids on the block; Charu Sharma, Deepika Deshpande and Rituraj were our very first colleagues. There were no real TV professionals at that point and those of us in theatre and the arts were much sought after to create new shows, some originals and a few rip-offs of globally ranked programmes adapted for the Indian market at a hundredth of the cost. *Tol Mol Ke Bol* was one of the first successful game shows that we produced for ZEE TV, along with *Newsline* for EL TV, a soap opera based on the politics and power of a media house which would be equally relevant two decades later. *Melting Pot* and *The Indian Spice Trail* were food shows long before food became a popular entertainment idiom; the shows were dubbed across languages and telecast in India, Africa, Singapore and the Far East. *Footprints on Water* and *Cool Talk Café* were amongst the first talk shows focused on artistes and innovators. *Choona Laga Ke* was a satire with puppets and muppets as characters designed by Dadi Pudumjee and scripted by a host of talented writers overseen by Mohit Satyanand, Teamwork's co-founder. There was also an innovative quiz show on BITV, shaped by Joy Bhattacharjya and Sudha Sadanand, commissioned by Mala Singh, and a slew of documentaries and social awareness films for UNICEF, Voluntary Health Association of India, the Ministry of Health and others. All of these kept us on the proverbial treadmill throughout the year.

Our schedules were punishing: early morning call times, mad dashes through Delhi's chaotic roads, script meetings, rehearsals and then three-camera shoots on the sound stage, trying to maximize the amount of content we could record in a day, given the non-existent budgets that TV afforded. U-Matic tapes had given way to Betacam technology which was expensive, as were camera and studio rentals, editing suites, the abundant food service, and the fees for actors, anchors, script writers, technicians, and lighting and camera crews.

Channels survived off their producers with ninety-day payment terms post telecast, which invariably stretched way beyond the contracted period, and you had to beg and cajole to be paid. Every Saturday afternoon, Mohit and I met our directors, producers and writers over samosas and tea to discuss themes and scripts for the coming week, go over edit and delivery schedules, view casting tapes, tweak story lines, and occasionally write out actors who had been irregular or had behaved badly on set.

Manika and Sharupa were our senior directors on multiple shows. Manika had studied mass communication in Jamia Millia Islamia University and had gone on to work with a number of directors and TV productions before she joined us. Sharupa had arrived on a bicycle one day at our F5 Hauz Khas Enclave office, in a pair of shorts, looking for a job. An actor in the Delhi theatre company Act One, she spent her days working with us and evenings rehearsing. They were the backbone of Teamwork Films along with our many other colleagues and were key to our mainstream productions. One afternoon, they came in exhausted, pleading that we should rethink our plans to continue in television. In those early days, we had to physically courier our tapes for tech checks to the channels in Mumbai or Delhi, and they, in turn, sent them on to Kathmandu for broadcast due to complex broadcasting laws in the country. Television knew no excuse, you couldn't pause for date night, nor for an illness, death or marriage. The weekly and daily shows had to be delivered, and delivered on schedule. The pace we worked at was relentless and unforgiving and the rewards questionable.

Mohit and I agreed that it was time to step off the treadmill. At any rate, television wasn't paying: the non-ending cycle of unpaid dues meant that we were in debt more often than not, barely keeping ahead of our monthly payments. At the time we were banking on the balance payments owed to us by the channels and the start of the new Onida TV Awards project to keep us afloat till we cracked a new opportunity. As they say, the best laid plans of mice and men invariably come to naught! Despite the channels threatening us with non-payment of our dues, we stopped our TV work and concentrated on full-length historical documentaries and the excitement of creating new products in the events space.

The first Onida TV Awards was the gold standard of awards! Hundreds of guests—actors and writers, directors and producers, channel heads and cinematographers, editors and technicians—were flown into Delhi. While the nominations had been announced in Mumbai to generate interest and shine a spotlight on brand Onida and the newly minted awards, the final event was held at Delhi's Taj Palace Hotel where the banquet hall accommodated up to 1,000 people. A fleet of luxury cars, buffet spreads, round-the-clock bars and personalized Onida monitors and TV sets were set up for the members of the 'academy' to view the nominations and cast their votes in the run-up to the final night.

It was spectacular! The awards were perceived to be credible, glamorous and exciting—and not coloured by influence or money. The fifty–fifty weightage for jury and academy votes meant that we had both industry peers and a considered jury coming together to celebrate the best in television. The post-awards party, fuelled by the best alcohol, went on through the night. Hundreds of invitees missed their flight connections back home the next morning despite production and travel assistants banging on doors and asking the hotel staff to help them wake the guests up from their alcoholic haze.

Once the dust had settled, reviews done and plans for the next year sorted, we decided to take our colleagues for an off-site celebration and bonding camp. Two busloads of people, including our circle of friends and family, set off for the Himalayan River Runners camp, which we had booked out to ensure we could accommodate the entire tribe. We sang, drank, danced, gossiped and ate our way to the camp with multiple roadside breaks for parathas and pakoras, milkshakes and beer. One long road trip later, we tumbled out of the bus, lugged our luggage, booze, comfort snacks and iceboxes packed with kebabs and tikkas, ham, bacon and cheese down the hill where we were greeted by familiar faces and Yousuf and Ganeve's trademark hospitality. The dining tent had been laid out with flasks of chai and biscuits, namkeen and pakoras. Guests were shown their camping sites and, most importantly, the toilet tents: sewage pits dug at the end of the campsite with commodes set above them, and rudimentary shower stalls attached to hammams that were lit in the morning for those brave enough to brace the chill in the air.

Daybreak was magical: the mist of the river outlined by the unbroken green speckled with red, the stunning flowers of the Flame of the Forest on the far bank, the sun cheekily peeping out from behind the hills to banish the night and reclaim its place as the all-powerful, all-nurturing giver of light and life. Post breakfast, we were packed into jeeps and driven 16 km upstream to pick up our rafts for the journey down the river, past Lakshman Jhula at Rishikesh. Our friends Tarun and Geetan (Tejpal) and their children Tiya and Cara were with us on this trip. Aditya, Tiya, Cara and Avik were fitted out with baby helmets and life jackets, only to be told that they were too young to make the entire journey and would have to drive down and join us at Three Blind

Mice, a somewhat milder rapid. Disappointed and teary eyed, they were escorted back to the jeep, while we were put through the paces and taught to row in unison and reminded to follow safety protocols and pull hard when asked to—or we would be stuck forever in a whirlpool.

A slew of rafts had been lined up for our use by the advance team, twelve seated in the larger ones and eight in the smaller ones. Our life jackets were strapped on, then tightened and tested to ensure they wouldn't ride over our heads should we fall into the river, and paddles in hand, we were onboarded. The Wall was the largest and most challenging of the rapids, and came right at the starting point of the course. It changed constantly, depending on the volume of water that hit the gigantic boulder; it carved out a hollow where invariably the raft flipped if you didn't pull in unison and you got caught in the backdraft, locked into a whirlpool, breaking free from which required extraordinary effort. As the raft was tossed into the air, you had to lean forward and bring to bear all your collective weight so that it balanced and landed right side up in the water, and then you had to row with all your might to get through the hole to the other side or be trapped in the whirlpool.

The first raft with Tarun Laroia, Yamini, Deepika, Niharika, Chandana and Rahul headed out to the centre and, despite their furious paddling, was tossed high in the air. Most of the rafters were thrown out.

Rahul Sen, our go-to colleague for everything finance and legal, had followed every instruction to a T and still managed to land face first and proceeded to drink the waters of the Ganga as he floated down. Yamini clambered up a rock and clung to it for dear life, swearing that there was no way she would ever get off that rock and go back into the river and that she should be left there forever to die. Deepika Gandhi, who had joined our production team and was affectionately called 'Chuttu', had thankfully surfaced, buoyed by her life jacket, and sailed down the river happily, while Chandana Chauhan bobbed in the water, white as a sheet with a slash of red from her lipstick, surfacing every now and then as she spluttered to catch a breath, too frightened to even scream. Tarun and Niharika managed to clamber to safety downstream and were thankfully none the worse for the experience.

Our raft was next out and as we hit the rapid and flew into the air, Viraj, the original stud muffin, began rowing furiously without his paddle even once touching the water—and in doing so, hit my head with his oar, leaving me momentarily dazed. Luckily, we didn't flip and most of us managed to stay on board. As was tradition, when we passed the Rollercoaster and approached Three Blind Mice, we jumped off and floated down the river in our wetsuits, exhilarated by the exercise, enjoying the warmth of the sun on our faces, the water enveloping us in its embrace, washing away our sins on its winding journey to the sea.

The Ganga is sacred. King Bhagiratha, whose ancestors were cursed by a sage and burnt to ashes, performed a penance and asked Lord Shiva to bring the river Ganga to earth to purify the ashes of his ancestors and liberate their souls. Lord Shiva agreed and asked the Goddess Ganga to descend to earth. Knowing that the power and might of her descent would destroy everything in its path, he embraced her in the coils of his dreadlocks and let her fall gently to earth where she washed over the ashes of the dead, redeeming them and giving them moksha. Hindus believe that a deceased's ashes must be immersed in the Ganga for their soul to find salvation. Upstream, at the confluence of the Bhagirathi and the Ganga, lie Rudraprayag and Karnaprayag, holy sites where the dead are brought from surrounding villages and cremated. Those with the resources pile up wood and offer ghee and sacred samagri as they light the pyres. Sadly, families that cannot afford the cost of the funeral and the wood consign half-burnt bodies to the river, which then float downstream, bloated and disfigured.

Rafting under the Lakshman Jhula is a special experience as you see a stream of pilgrims peering over and looking at the boats go by, pausing a moment to pray or feed the fish, marvelling at the myth of the building of the bridge; it is believed that Shravan Kumar balanced his blind and aged parents on either shoulder as they set out on a pilgrimage and crossed a bridge of ropes over the turbulent river at this point.

Partly dazed from the hit on my head and lulled into a trance by the warmth of the midday sun on my face, I was drifting along when I suddenly began feeling uncomfortable. Looking around, I spotted a half-burnt, distended corpse floating by me. I swam away towards the landing beach, conscious of a chilling energy that seemed to want to overpower me. We pulled up our rafts, undid our life jackets, handed over our paddles and headed to the jeeps waiting to take us back to the campsite.

In the mountains, night comes upon you suddenly—a shroud of darkness is pulled across the face of the sun as it dips behind a mountain. You look up hoping to spot the moon and with it the first star, a sign of good luck upon which you can wish, and then spot the second and third stars as the night pours in its inky blackness, painting out the day and claiming the universe.

The fire was lit. Val (Valentine) Shipley, who, along with Mohit and Kanika, had set up Friends of Music and was our go-to person for any musical intervention, and who boasted of a gorgeous voice and a childlike innocence, brought the night alive with music—Queen's

'I Want to Break Free', the Moody Blues' 'Nights in White Satin', the Eagles' 'Hotel California', and a lot of Pink Floyd. On any other occasion, I would have been belting out those numbers with Val, being the heart and soul of the party. But that night, I sat alone in a faraway tent, clutching a bottle of vodka in one hand, still feeling disoriented and not quite myself.

Puneeta had fed the kids, and Pushpa didi had tucked them into bed. Even though I heard Puneeta calling for me, I remained in the shadow of the tent, grappling with deep, dark emotions which seemed to have taken over my being. Given my surliness and off-hand dismissal of her concern, Puneeta went back to the fire. The moon and the stars in the night sky played hide-and-seek with the clouds, plunging the area into darkness and then suddenly bathing it in moonshine. At some point in the night, I staggered back, barely conscious of the surroundings, and got into my sleeping bag. All through the remainder of the night, I tossed and turned in discomfort, drifting in and out of nightmares with a vague sense of the unease that had engulfed me earlier.

Morning came swiftly as the earth spun towards a new day, the sky changing from an inky blue to the orange and crimson hues of marigold flowers and pink carnations dusted in gold and sprinkled with morning dew. Still groggy from the vodka, my temple throbbing painfully where I had been hit, I felt the unease of the previous night sweep over me in a tsunami of despair, cutting away the light and joy of a new dawn, and making me want to avoid stepping out into the sunshine. There was no lightness of being, no happiness, no joy in being greeted by Puneeta or in seeing the kids or our friends. I stayed in our tent for as long as I could, zipped inside my sleeping bag, avoiding the breakfast area, clinging to my bottle of vodka, hoping that there would be something there that would lighten this overwhelming despair that had numbed my soul, shrouded my mind and plunged me into a dark crevice.

When it was time to leave, we were shepherded to the two waiting buses. As I boarded the bus, I could hear a voice saying, 'Main aa raha hoon (I am coming)!' I tried to block out the voice in my head with even more vodka, but it only grew louder and more insistent, crowding out every thought till I screamed in panic for the bus to stop and for our kids to be sent to the one behind us. Puneeta, though completely perplexed by what was happening, refused to leave my side.

As the bus stopped for a pit break, I felt an invisible force lead me down the steps and into the oncoming speeding traffic, only to be stopped by Tarun who bundled me back into the bus. At this point, the bus driver apparently announced that I was possessed and asked everyone to get back in. Voices filled my head, tearing at my chest, driving the breath out of my body and terrifying me till I blanked out.

What happened next was related to me by Puneeta, Tarun, Geetan, Mohit and Viraj over many days and has become a staple story in our vast pantheon of tales. It seems that I would sit still for a while and then suddenly hurl myself into the air, breaking free of their grip, limbs flailing, my whole body convulsing. Val had ducked for cover under a seat at the back of the bus while Larry (Sanjeev Laroia, our company's chartered account and friend), Viraj, Mohit and Tarun tried to keep me pinned down. I would appear to be calm and seemingly normal and wait for them to relax their grip momentarily, at which point I would fly off the seat again and again with the unfamiliar strength of one who is possessed.

The bus stopped at a local hospital in Haridwar where the doctors administered an injection to sedate me. The bus driver, fearful for his own safety, wanted to get to the end of this frightening journey, while Viraj, being Viraj, chomped away on a dozen samosas, his knee placed firmly on my chest.

The seven-hour bus journey from Rishikesh and Haridwar to Delhi via Roorkee and Meerut was interminable and exhausting. When we arrived in Delhi, I was taken straight to Aashlok Hospital at Safdarjung Enclave for an EEG, but it showed nothing; I insisted on going home rather than being admitted for observation into a sterile hospital room.

Over the next two weeks, I wasn't quite in my senses. I would stare vacantly at the ceiling or sit listlessly on the rooftop while friends took turns to keep me company between their own daily chores of office and home. I registered little. Day and night merged into one with an intense sense of darkness and unease accompanied by occasional suicidal urges overwhelming me. My mind had shut down—symptomatic of a breakdown. At Dhanda and Shalini's reception in Chattarpur, I wandered away from the guests to find a quiet space, instructed by the voice in my head which would pop up every now and then. Puneeta, Geetan and Tarun, who had gone off to get drinks, panicked when they realized I wasn't there. They searched the entire venue and found me in the nick of time, just as I was headed out to the road and into the oncoming traffic.

Mohit was seriously concerned about my mental health and the future of our company; he gathered our colleagues and told them that this could be a long haul, and that everyone would need to be supportive.

Puneeta arranged to meet with Arvinder, from Sanjeevini, a counselling facility set up by a group of mental health specialists, who, upon hearing my back story, including my association with the Salaam Baalak

Trust, asked gently: 'So why do you feel the need to give back and help others?' It wasn't quite the question I was expecting or could deal with at the time, and I mumbled something about the inequity around us, how it was an unfair world that mistreated those who had no access to resources and how it was the responsibility of each of us to help those less fortunate and bridge the inequity gap.

That first session did nothing to alleviate my condition, and I fought the nights, afraid to sleep lest the voice return. A week passed and then ten full days. And then, bored of being consumed by the dreariness that comes with illness, I snapped out of it—the voice in my head seemed to have gone and I made peace with the spirit I had encountered and got straight back to the hustle and bustle of daily life.

Was I possessed? Was it a mental breakdown, a natural shutting down of my mind that needed time and space to heal? But then how could you explain the superhuman strength that I had experienced, or the sense of having a soul possess me? And what indeed of my miraculous recovery? Looking back, it's still difficult to decipher what happened, and as for Arvinder's pointed question about 'why I needed to help others', who knows, as I am still in search of that answer.

7

An Accident Foretold

Goa

Each spring, prior to the Navratras, the nine-day celebration of Goddess Jagadhatri, or Shakti or Durga, Shashtriji came to visit us. It was my sister-in-law Poonam who first suggested that we meet with him. A devotee of Tirupati with a deeply held belief in the occult, she used to consult him for his ability to determine a person's future by reading their face.

Shashtriji visited the office twice a year and we typically talked about the future of the world, what was in store for India, who would win the elections and, invariably, I would ask about the health and future of our sons. Aditya, Shashtriji said, would be into computers and would always live by the sea west of us—he was then obsessed with the Xbox, and went on to learn various forms of martial arts and set up his training studio and residential programme, Light Haven, in Goa. Shashtriji divined that Avik would go abroad but would return and remain by our side. And that's what he did. He went to Hampshire College, Massachusetts, to study, and returned to volunteer time with Puneeta's Yuva Ekta Foundation, interned at the Planning Commission of India, and then joined Teamwork to curate and programme some of our music and heritage festivals apart from pursuing his own musical journey which includes composing, teaching, acting and performing in a number of different bands.

Shashtriji said I would live till the age of ninety-two or ninety-three(!) and that at seventy-two I might have an 'ummm' moment from which I would recover. At Teamwork, it would be slow going—'Papad belna hain, koi labh nahin milega. Koi aur hota toh kab ka band kar deta (You'll work with little gain. Anyone else in a similar predicament would have shut shop long ago).' Shani was upon me, and I should steer clear of meat, drink and sex on Thursdays; he, in turn, would do a forty-five-day puja to ward off the evil effects of this malevolent planet.

Well, puja or no puja, the universe has been kind to us and I am always thankful for the opportunity to do what I do. Many of our colleagues continue to consult Shashtriji about their future, their fortunes, health, families and love lives. He meets five people a day as that seems to be within his capacity to divine the future and make sense of the past.

In 1996, Shashtriji came to see me towards the end of April. Once we had sorted out the state of the world, he casually asked, 'Where will you be in early June?' I told him we holidayed in Goa each summer as it was our favourite destination. We body-surfed on the waves at the Taj Aguada, and visited our favourite haunts, including Suza Lobo, Bob's Inn and Sea Shell, gorging on butter garlic calamari, Goan prawn curry and king fish recheado, lounging through the day at the local beach shacks, Hello Brothers and Jolly Boys, where the kids ordered up a mountain of chilli paneer or fried fish, chips and strawberry milkshakes. Each year, apart from Tarun, Geetan, Tiya, Cara and Manika and Viraj, we were joined by an ever-growing tribe of extended family and friends.

Intrigued as to why Shashtriji was concerned about our holiday, I asked after the reason and he replied, 'Nahin, nahin, koi khaas baat nahin hain (No, no, just asking, nothing you should be concerned about really).' He then went on to suggest that we consider cancelling our holiday plans. When I asked him why, he repeated, 'Nahin, nahin, kuch aisi baat nahin, bas poochh raha hoon jaane ki kya zaroorat hai (No, no, nothing of concern, I was just checking why you need to go there).' As the conversation progressed, he asked where we would be on the sixth of June. I said I had no idea, apart from the fact that we would be in Goa, probably at the Taj Holiday Village. He suggested that perhaps on that day, we should consider staying indoors and not move out of the hotel. He went on to mention that his guru had asked him to visit me specially to find out our plans and to tell us to be cautious on the sixth of June. On asking him to explain why we had to be cautious, Shashtriji continued to be evasive, and repeated that there wasn't anything to worry about really, all we needed to do was be careful. He then announced that he would perform a special forty-five-day puja as an 'upay' (a solution to the supposed problem) and left. Barring paying for the annual puja he performed, I seldom took serious note of what Shashtriji said and rarely heeded his counsel, and so it was that in the hurdy-gurdy of everyday life in Delhi, I totally forgot about our conversation.

Goa is paradise! As the plane banks over the Mandovi and Zuari rivers in the final descent to Dabolim airport, perched on a plateau garlanded by palm trees and dotted with new constructions, a sense of calm and peace descends upon you.

In 1986, Puneeta and I had spent our honeymoon at the Taj Aguada, a welcome break from the ten-day extended wedding celebration with the usual outpouring of love, politics and drama that is inevitable in any great big Indian wedding. It was everything a romantic destination should be. Evenings spent sitting outside our villa and gazing upon the inky blue expanse of the Arabian Sea under a starlit sky. Day trips to explore the Saturday market in faraway Mapusa with the scent of freshly ground spices, gur and dried fish heavy in the air, strings of homemade Goan chorizo, necklaces of chillies strung together, aromatic salts mixed with ginger or garlic, pepper and chilli arranged invitingly on wooden carts. We visited the churches of Old Goa and the night markets of Anjuna and Baga, danced at the carnival, partied with Puneeta's cousin Deepak and his partner, whom we met at the hotel, and then proceeded to trawl through delightful pubs and shacks and soak in the sun and sand. Back in the 1980s, Calangute and Candolim were pockets of quiet, with vast acres of empty beach dotted with the occasional shack and no hint of the tourist avalanche that would eventually take over the state.

To return ten years later with the kids and our friends to the Taj Holiday Village was, in many ways, akin to coming home. Our holidays had their own rhythm, well steeped in laughter, drinks, bonhomie and stories. The kids woke up early and paddled in the children's pool. I would emerge closer to lunchtime and we would then shift base to the beach house. Numerous vodkas later, we would catch an afternoon nap and then, having deposited the four kids at the children's activity centre under the supervision of the Taj staff, we would head out to take in the magic of Goa with the help of cherry and whiskey sours over sweet No. 9 Vinicola, and gorge on pork sorpotel, prawn recheado and beef chilli fry.

The morning of 6 June began as any other, with a late brunch of dosas, bacon and sausages at Caravela, the Taj Holiday Village beach shack, followed by body surfing in the Arabian Sea, vodka sours and mounds of butter garlic calamari and Goan fish curry for lunch. As evening approached, we sent the kids to the play-centre and left for Bom Successo, a nearby watering hole where much wine was drunk and the problems of the world discussed. As the night drew on, a heated discussion around the merits of buying or borrowing books erupted between Tarun and Geetan and ended with Puneeta throwing an empty plastic bottle at Tarun. Annoyed at the racket we were making, the guests at the next table complained to the owner who came down and asked all of us to leave the restaurant. It was 11 p.m. and as we got up to leave, we heard a loud crash. Instinctively, we looked around to check if everyone was all right and then rushed out to see what had happened. The first rains of the season had broken and the mist had settled. The two gentlemen who had complained about us had crashed their bike and were out cold on the road, the bike's wheels spinning in the air. I took the wrist of the taller gentleman and, unable to find a pulse, declared him dead, only for him to let out a drunken snore. His name was David and he was 6 feet 2 inches or thereabouts and must have weighed at least 120 kg. His friend picked himself up and set about lamenting their fate and sharing with us how they had come down from Ooty.

We picked David up, staggering under his weight, hailed a passing cab and instructed the driver to take the two gentlemen to the closest primary healthcare centre. We followed on our bikes. While we waited for the doctor, I instructed the girls that David shouldn't be given a sedative and that they should continuously speak to him to keep him engaged and try to gauge if he had suffered an injury to the brain, all of this based on some information I had picked up somewhere about first aid in head injury cases. When the doctor appeared with an injection, the girls objected and said this was not good medical practice. The somewhat sleepy doctor, annoyed at being woken up, demanded to know who they were to advise him on what to do, and then proceeded to give David an injection and treat his cuts and bruises.

Tarun and I had meanwhile escaped the humidity and dust of the crumbling medical outpost and were leaning against a car on the main road, chatting about the incident, when the Taj duty manager who was passing by spotted us and stopped to ask what had happened. He suggested that we head back to the hotel and said that he would ferry the patient to Bambolim General Hospital, a forty-five-minute drive from where we were. It was well past midnight by then, and we were all stone-cold sober thanks to the accident. Tarun and Geetan got onto their scooter with Puneeta riding pillion behind them. Viraj and Manika got onto the second bike with me hanging on at the back. Just as we were about to head out, Puneeta jumped off Tarun's scooter, came over to me and suggested that we swap places, which we did. Tarun cautioned Viraj about speeding, given the rains and the slippery roads, as he shot off into the dark.

The mist had reduced visibility; there were just a few streetlights and the shops were shut. Manika warned Puneeta to hang on to her regardless of what happened and to not let go. She had long suffered Viraj's rash driving. Once, when they were returning from Fireball, the popular disco at 32nd Milestone in Gurgaon that we all frequented, he had turned the corner near Aya Nagar in his ambassador at great speed and the door had swung open and Manika was flung out of the car. Oblivious to what had happened, Viraj had continued to talk to her for some time before realizing she wasn't there. He had turned back to look for her, only to find her sitting on the side of the road, bleeding profusely, her skin shredded from the impact of falling out of the car.

Tarun, who was a cautious driver, drove the scooter with care. As we approached the turning to the Taj Holiday Village gate, we saw a bike lying on its side, the wheels still spinning, with three bodies strewn across the road. Viraj and Manika seemed relatively unhurt, but Puneeta had hit her head on the road when she fell off the scooter and was haemorrhaging, blood gushing from the wound. By now we knew the drill and raced to the hotel reception, got hold of a hotel car and asked the front desk to let the Bambolim hospital know we were headed there. Tarun and I left with Puneeta, leaving Manika and Viraj to clean up and check if they had any cuts or injuries, and Geetan to keep an eye on the kids and reassure them that all was well.

At the Bambolim General Hospital, we wheeled Puneeta into emergency, only to find David being treated by the duty doctor on one bed. On another bed was the Bom Successo owner who had followed his guests to the hospital and had run into a herd of buffaloes in the dark, injuring his knees and elbows. On a third bed lay the Taj duty manager, moaning in pain. He had fallen into a ditch while helping with David's stretcher, and had ended up with a broken toe.

The emergency doctor and the nurses were perplexed at the sudden influx of patients who all seemed to know each other but had arrived at different times and had been involved in three separate accidents. Having examined Puneeta, the doctor instructed the nurse to stitch her head wound to stem the bleeding. As the nurse began shaving Puneeta's head, a fountain of blood erupted. She then plunged what looked like a harpoon into Puneeta's scalp. From across the table, Tarun looked at me with an oh-my-god-is-this-for-real expression just as I rolled my eyes and passed out cold in slow motion, straight out of a comic book scene, the doctor yelling for me to be taken out and Tarun cracking up at the image.

It was now 3 a.m. Puneeta had been patched up, and we followed the nurse as she wheeled the stretcher through the blue and cream corridors to the ICU. Viraj had arrived from the hotel, freshly bathed and dressed in white socks, T-shirt and shorts. He came bounding in with great energy and equal parts guilt. The ICU was built in an L shape with the vast nurses' table—crowded with syringe trays, medication, reports, blood pressure machines and more—along the x-axis. Deciding he needed to take a shortcut, Viraj attempted to leap over it, crashing into the table and taking it down with him. The quiet of the ICU was shattered as heart-and-lung machines stopped momentarily and patients were jolted awake as their pulleys and weights shifted and creaked; every emergency alarm went off in the silence of the night.

It took a while for the chaos to die down and for Puneeta to be transferred from the stretcher to the bed. I asked Tarun and Viraj to head back to the hotel and said I would keep vigil till the morning; we would rearrange our plans to leave for Delhi. I have never been one for general wards or emergency rooms, and as dawn broke and I looked around, I realized that the beds around me had patients in various stages of trauma. In the next bed lay an elderly man whose colostomy bag had leaked. That was enough for me to march off to admissions and ask for Puneeta to be discharged. My reckoning was that she would be much better off with medical care in the cool climes of our Taj Village room than in a general hospital; and if she were to die, well then, it would in the comfort of a luxurious bed far away from the sights and smells of an ugly ICU.

It took us a few days to receive a clearance to fly Puneeta back to Delhi where her MRI scan showed a major lesion and trauma to her brain. Thereafter began the inevitable visits to the doctors and consultations with neurologists and neurosurgeons. Dr Ravi Bhatia, the head of the neuroscience department at AIIMS, wanted Puneeta to begin a regime of medication for six months and instructed her to avoid swimming, driving, climbing steps or walking on her own. Puneeta would have none of it and went off to her family homoeopath, the legendary Dr Chopra. The impact of the accident and the resulting injury had clearly triggered her impatience and bouts of anger. The tedious questions from Dr Chopra—who was then in his late eighties—had her flying off the handle at regular intervals and I had to step in and negotiate her responses. It took almost a year for her to recover, though her short-term memory was permanently impacted, as was her patience. Amidst all of this, Aditya came up to me and asked if I was planning to grow my hair. I just hadn't had the time to go to Affinity, the hair salon in Greater Kailash II. I asked him why. And he responded that were I to grow my hair, I couldn't come to his school as it would attract too much attention. That was the magic moment when I decided to grow out my hair and avoid parent-teacher meetings and other school responsibilities. And the rest, as they say, is history!

Some weeks later, Shashtriji returned to check on us. He said that he had tried to ward off the worst through a series of pujas. It seemed that while you couldn't change your destiny, you could try and deflect it through various upays! Had I been on the bike that crashed, the consequences would have been far worse, he said; I would have lost a limb or injured an organ. As a wife is the only person who could take on a husband's karma,

Shashtriji had tried to orchestrate the same through his forty-five-day puja.

The sixth of June was a disastrous dasha or celestial time for me, which was why Shashtriji's guru had sent him to warn us of its consequences and find a way to reduce the impact of the planetary configurations.

Shashtriji continues to visit me twice a year at the office and has made a number of predictions since then that have come to pass.

8

The Fire

Safdarjung Enclave, New Delhi

A quarter moon hung listlessly in a star-smudged sky. A power outage had snuffed out the lights. Not a leaf moved in the shimmering heat of that June night.

I climbed out of bed and peered intently into the darkness, hoping to see what had triggered the shutdown. Was it a short circuit in the area or had our own electricity connection tripped, overloaded by multiple air conditioners humming in quiet contentment?

I hated summers; despite the promises of the Delhi Electric Supply Undertaking (DESU) each year, the creaking system of the 1990s just couldn't cope with the demand, and so we lived in eternal dread of sudden power cuts.

Our house in Safdarjung Enclave stood on the main east to west thoroughfare connecting Kamal Cinema to Africa Avenue.

Having finally retired from the government after birthing the nuclear submarine project, Pa hadn't wanted to move far from the centre of Delhi. He relished the comfort of Teen Murti Bhawan, where he was a fellow; the Delhi Gymkhana Club and the India International Centre were his go-to places between board meetings, seminars, his many writing projects and his office, the Indian Ocean Society near Qutub Institutional Area.

Safdarjung Enclave and the nearby village of Mohammadpur were home to historical monuments dating back to the Lodhi and Tughlaq periods. The architecture was mixed. The three-domed Teen Burjee or Tin Burj was from the fifteenth century, its architecture unlike that of tombs from other periods. The mausoleum of Nawab Auditullah Khan adjoined a monument known simply as the Tomb of Mohammadpur, heavily encroached-upon and just about surviving the vagaries of time and the expansion of an ever-growing city. A short distance away lay the much-weathered Bijri Khan Tomb. These were the burial grounds of the armies of the Lodhi and Tughlaq dynasties, many of the tombstones lost to the antiquities of time. The only remnants were the odd ghoul or ghost, compelled by fate to co-habit with graves, bats and rats.

The year was 1997. Inder Kumar Gujral had recently been sworn in as the prime minister of India. There was much rejoicing amongst Delhi's elite as he and his poet wife were 'people like us' and known to everyone, a genteel and much-welcomed addition to the corridors of power which had witnessed turmoil over the past few years. There was a collective sigh of relief and the hope that perhaps it would be business as usual after a messy if not embarrassing tryst with coalition politics.

Opposite our house, a clutch of pyjama kurta-clad neighbours had collected in front of DESU's somewhat ramshackle office with its vestiges of long-faded PWD-yellow walls stained with betel juice, to check when the electricity would be restored. I paced up and down, counting my steps in the corridor from the balcony to our bedroom, with hope and a prayer that the power would miraculously return, providing relief to the creaking fans running on the inverter.

Light burst upon us suddenly, illuminating the peepul tree and vanquishing every ghoul and spirit that had sought refuge there momentarily, before we were plunged right back into darkness. A groan ran through the crowd and voices took on a higher pitch, anger floating on half-digested kukad and rajma–chawal being belched out at the hapless DESU night staff. A few minutes later, the lights were back on and peace prevailed. The kurtas melted into the night and the road was given back to the stray dogs. Exhausted, I climbed back into bed. Puneeta hadn't stirred. A volcano could have erupted; an earthquake could have brought buildings tumbling down; a dust storm could have ripped out the peepul tree—but she would sleep through it all … a sleep of innocence and the sign of a peaceful soul.

I surfed a dream, tumbling into its dark crevices, and was jolted awake by the smell of burning rubber. I leapt out of bed to check on the power points in the house, walked down the corridor and looked at the meter box, its wires criss-crossed like Medusa's curls, glanced at the inverter and having found nothing out of order, went back to the comfort of my bed.

An acrid smell reminiscent of a funeral pyre clawing at dead flesh woke me up again. I scrambled to see what had caught fire, but nothing seemed to be amiss. A while later, the burning smell was back, only this time I could visualize the swirl of smoke, its stench nauseating and overpowering, making me light-headed and giddy. I prodded Puneeta awake, resentful of her ability to sleep through it all. The two of us checked every plug and power connection, the electricity meters, the fuse box and fridges, and found nothing. Puneeta threw my eye mask at me, handed me some

Amrutanjan balm to dab on my nostrils to block out the smell, asked me to cover my head with a pillow, hugged me tight and drifted off to sleep.

The next morning, when I related what had transpired, Puneeta shared her story. She and her colleague Urmila, then head of accounts at Perspective Films, had been experimenting with the occult for some time while working on *Shakti*, their programme for ZEE TV. They wanted to explore the many dimensions of healing. Both Urmila and Puneeta had taken a Reiki course. Over time, they had begun connecting with other energies and dimensions. After Urmila's father passed over, she made it a point to speak with him regularly, be it on family matters or just garnering advice and exploring life on the other side of the meridian. Much of this they did through planchette, as Urmila had some modest skill as a medium, and day after day, they invited passing souls through their Ouija board, peering into the past and hoping to foretell the future.

I used to freak out every time Puneeta and Urmila took out their Ouija board. This was no child's play and certainly not some timepass activity for amateurs. Dealing with souls from other dimensions meant you had a responsibility. While Puneeta and Urmila were in tune with these 'other energies' and were able to attract them and engage them in conversation, they hadn't quite mastered the art of sending them back into the light. On this fateful day, as they reached out, a traumatized soul in the form of a little girl came rushing through, engulfed in flames, frantic and terrified, trying to escape the lived tragedy that had consumed her and her family.

Earlier that day, in Green Park market, a stone's throw from our neighbourhood, the Uphaar cinema tragedy had played itself out. The blockbuster film *Border*, based on the Battle of Longewala during the 1971 Indo–Pak conflict, starring Sunny Deol, Suniel Shetty, Akshay Khanna and Jackie Shroff with Tabu and Rakhee among others, and directed by J.P. Dutta, was playing to full houses and there was a heavy rush at the box office. A transformer installed and maintained by the Delhi Vidyut Board had caught fire due to poor maintenance, and in the absence of an oil soak pit, the oil had spread and the fire had rapidly filled the cinema hall with smoke, suffocating those inside. (Fire and safety norms were routinely flouted and no building was really safe.) To make the situation worse, the hall's exit was padlocked to keep the crowd outside from rushing in and the fire exit was blocked—there was no emergency exit operational. As smoke filled the theatre, people began to try to flee, resulting in a stampede. Fifty-nine people lost their lives in the tragedy that day and over a hundred were injured. The Uphaar cinema management and the fire services took little responsibility for what had happened. Fire tenders worked through the day to douse the flames and save as many people as they could. Families across Delhi held their breath, waiting to see who had been rescued, their hopes diminishing as bodies were pulled out one by one.

The Krishnamurthys, whose two children had died in the Uphaar Tragedy (as it came to be known), set up an organization with the aim of seeking justice and compensation for the victims and holding to account those responsible for the disaster. Over the years, they fought a callous administration; the influential Ansal brothers who owned the cinema hall but wished to take no responsibility for what had happened; the fire department and other local government departments that had neglected routine checks and were bribed to look the other way. It took more than two decades for them to fight their way through the courts and through an obstructive bureaucracy till they were able to put in place some much-needed health and safety policies and provide compensation to the families who had been impacted.

The tragedy had occurred on Friday, the thirteenth. The morning after the tragedy, sitting out in the balcony, we witnessed four bodies shrouded in white being loaded into a truck from a building a few houses up the road. The family members were consoling one another;

we could hear the loud laments of the grandfather mourning the young lives that had been snuffed out way before their time.

The girl who had appeared to Puneeta and Urmila had lost her life in the Uphaar fire; she was terrified and in constant motion, running from the flames. At that time, Puneeta and Urmila hadn't quite fathomed the tragedy that had taken place and had tried to calm her down, but the girl wouldn't stay still, caught up in the horror that surrounded her, desperate to escape. They entreated her to move towards the light, sent her light and love to calm her, but she was too frantic to listen to them. They repeated their prayers, but to no avail. They ended their session and shut down the board, not quite realizing that the soul had found nowhere to go. The next morning, they meditated and sent her healing, love and light and helped her find a path to a new dimension.

I made Puneeta and Urmila promise that they wouldn't pull out the Ouija board again except under supervision. Thereafter, they began channelling their ascended master, Gurudev, reaching out to him for advice and help whenever they needed. Urmila passed over a few years later, after having set up the Karmic Research Centre (KRC), a sacred space for healing and spiritual empowerment now housed in Noida under Dilip Shankar's supervision.

Dilip, a former colleague at Teamwork in the nineties, had lost his father, Ajay Shankar, in an accident. Ajay had been on his way back from Shirdi when the driver of his car swerved to avoid a truck and collided with a stationary tractor trailer carrying sugarcane, a stick of which pierced Ajay's skull, causing instant death. Unable to deal with the tragedy, his family had come to the KRC to make sense of his sudden death and speak with him through Gurudev, to understand why he had died in this sudden and violent way.

Gurudev explained that Ajay had subconsciously been preparing himself to leave the world and it seems that in the months leading up to the accident, he had been reading books on the afterlife and related themes. Dilip, an empathetic and wise man, involved himself heart and soul in the KRC and its activities, much to the initial concern of his family who, over time, came to respect his decision; he and Puneeta continue to host meditation sessions, both in person in Noida and in our home in Gurgaon, and online.

The KRC helps people find their mojo, make sense of sickness and death, revisit their past and deal with the mundane: broken hearts and broken souls, problems at work or those of family, depression and mental health issues and other afflictions. They put out recorded meditations, run art and healing workshops and provide opportunities for those wishing to explore their inner spiritual journey—and in doing so hope to understand their past patterns and control dramas, take responsibility for their choices and the resultant consequences, and 'let go' as they forgive those who may have hurt them knowingly or unknowingly, and seek forgiveness from those who may have been hurt because of their actions, so that in the act of 'letting go', they heal themselves, their past and their present.

9

The Spirit of the Mountains

Nainital, Switzerland, Ladakh

In 1999, during one of our many mountain getaways, Tarun and Geetan, who were always in search of an ideal piece of land to acquire, chanced upon a lovely plot spread across a ridge adjacent to a small village called Gethia in Nainital district. The nearby sanctuary had been a haven for those suffering from tuberculosis and needing to 'take the air'. Overlooking Nainital on one side and the deep valleys of the Garhwal on the other, the land was dotted with trees and had an old colonial stone house, the refuge of a

Madam Durell who had lived and died there and had supposedly hosted Mahatma Gandhi for tea when he stopped by once.

Tarun and Geetan fell in love with the derelict old building and its stunning location and took us there to see it. The house itself was just a shell—the wooden floors had long succumbed to the combined depredations of the weather and villagers who came in search of wood to light their hearths, and the roof was a tangle of half-broken tiles. Its formidable stone walls, however, were two feet thick and impenetrable. It boasted of one pretend loo, a hole in the outhouse over which you had to squat, gingerly balancing yourself so as not to fall into a pile of aged potty.

Over the next ten years, Tarun and Geetan restored the house, creating an enclosed wraparound balcony which became a sit-out to play cards and table tennis, drink, swap stories and discuss current issues in; they added rooms and re-laid the gardens and planted scores of trees. Each summer, winter, monsoon and spring, we gathered as a tribe to holiday there, setting up camp, holding open umbrellas at night to avoid getting totally soaked by the rain pouring in through the broken roof. Our days were filled with the constant hammering (which we labelled thoka-thaki) by the local workers who were fixing the roof, constructing balconies, opening up stone walls, putting in bay windows, polishing the floors, and setting up modern amenities, including a heated pool—until finally it seemed to be ready!

We brought in the millennium with a monumental celebration, a gathering of family and friends who poured in from all over. We played walking the plank—a midnight dare, where you walked over the yet-to-be-nailed-down beams of wood to take a leak, spilling out into the night sky and communing with nature.

Despite the promise of a good time that Two Chimneys (as the house is called) held, whenever Puneeta and I drove up to it, we felt a 'presence', initially angry and aggressive at the thought that intruders had stepped into a sacred space that once belonged to Madam Durell, but later a more benign and welcoming presence as the spirit must have realized that no one meant any harm to her or her homestead. Puneeta felt that the old lady wanted reassurance and suggested that a plaque commemorating Madam Durell be placed in a prominent place in the house.

Kailash and his efficient wife, Manju, managed the bookings and supervised the estate. They, along with the other staff members, had grown to accept the spirit's presence and weren't shocked by her occasional appearances. Madam Durell mostly kept to herself, sometimes hovering around the property, peeping into the former goat shed, which had been converted into a comfortable suite of rooms with a bay window looking out onto the garden. Her favourites seemed to be the Olive and Oak rooms, located one above the other. One night, a guest woke up in the bunk bed in the Oak room and saw an old lady peering in through the skylight. Terrified, he ran out of the room, screaming the house down, and refused to go back in, unconvinced by the house staff's assurances that the apparition didn't mean any harm.

On one particular visit to Two Chimneys, having settled in to sleep after the long drive, I got up to use the loo, and noticed a lady in a loose white chemise with a full head of silver hair peering at us from the corner of the room. She, unlike many other spirits that I had encountered, appeared peaceful. She didn't seem to mind being spotted and was in no hurry to disappear. She hung about, more like floated around for a bit, gazing at me, Puneeta and Gunjan, Geetan's sister who was also in the room, and then gently faded away.

I wasn't frightened; I felt a sense of comfort the way you do when you meet a friend. I wondered if the legendary Madam Durell wished to engage with her guests as she may have done when she was alive. Gunjan also spotted her when she woke up to go to the loo, and once again the apparition stayed awhile before fading away.

Over the years, she has often been spotted on the roof, peering through the skylight, or just drifting through the corridors and the rooms, perhaps happy to have her house restored and resplendent with teak and oak furniture, bookshelves and four-poster beds, and to hear the pitter-patter of feet and the sound of tea being poured into cups and saucers, and to see cricket being played on the lawns and goldfish swim in the pond outside the Olive room.

There is something about the mountains and the way they tend to be an abode for spirits, irrespective of geography or location. In 2022, Shams, a festival producer and colleague from Teamwork, and I were on a visit to Berne to explore the possibility of setting up 'India in the Alps', a new multi-arts festival, in Switzerland. The Indian ambassador to Switzerland, Sanjay Bhattacharya, had been the former ambassador in Egypt, where he and his wife, Ranu, an Indian classical dancer by profession, had seen first-hand how creativity and innovation could be leveraged as smart power to build links with governments, businesses, locals, influencers and the arts community. While India on the Nile was a long-running festival in Egypt, established jointly by Ambassador Navdeep Suri and us, growing into the largest and most exciting international festival in the country, with editions in cities like Cairo, Alexandria, Port Said, Sharm El Sheikh and Hurghada, the festival in Switzerland would be a new venture with open-air performances, gala dinners, talks, concerts, exhibitions and a display of craft presented in Zurich, Berne and Geneva.

The Indian ambassador's residence in Berne is located in Brunnadern, a stylish part of town on the outskirts of the city. The Swiss capital city has quaint paved streets with steel and stone bridges spanning the Aare River, the longest river in Switzerland originating at the Oberaar glacier and running through the lake-town of Brienz and past the castle of Thun before circling the capital city. Berne is famous for its heritage tower, the Zytglogge, built in 1191, and the astronomical clock added three centuries later, in 1530. Till the nineteenth century, everyone in the region set their watches as per this clock. Every hour, on the hour, this 500-year-old masterpiece comes alive with its many wonderful figurines who march about, making it a key attraction for visitors to the city.

One warm summer night, we headed to the guest annexe at the ambassador's residence. The two-storeyed cottage, which stood independent of the main house, had its own suite of rooms and opened up to the forest at the back that ran all the way down to the river. The heritage property had been acquired by the Indian government in 1949 and had been renovated over time. Like most Swiss homes, it didn't have fans or any other cooling system.

Even if the days were warm, the evenings were mostly cool and pleasant, except for this particular June night which was uncomfortably hot. Unused to a temperature differential of more than a few degrees on either side of 20 degrees Celsius, I had thrown open all the windows and doors in the bedroom to allow the mountain breeze to blow through and cool the place.

It was a full moon night and light flooded the room. I wondered briefly about shutting the windows, lest a wild animal come through, and drawing the curtains to cut out the light, but then decided to don my eye mask and drifted off to sleep to the sound of a barn owl hooting in the distance and the occasional yipping of foxes on the prowl.

I was in the midst of a dream, mostly about Chinese food, when I woke up with a start, sensing that someone was in the room. A sprightly gent with an immaculately combed goatee in brown tinged with white, sporting khaki-coloured trousers and a twill jacket, doffed his Swiss peak cap, complete with a feather, leaned forward and said a very terse 'hello'. Terrified, I leapt out of bed, rushed to the other end of the large bedroom and turned on the light. Breathing heavily and still frightened, I turned around to confront the intruder, only to find that he had disappeared.

I padded down the corridor to see if my colleague Shams was awake—and check if the person had gone into one of the other rooms. Shams's door was shut and it appeared that he was fast asleep. I went from room to room, turning on the lights and looking inside cupboards, behind doors and under the beds, and then proceeded to shut every window in the cottage before returning to my room with a great deal of trepidation. After checking the room and its many alcoves and cupboards again, I decided to leave a light on, put on my eye mask and added a pillow on top of my head to stop the light from coming in and tried to go back to sleep, with little success.

In the morning, I asked Ranu if she had ever seen a ghost or spirit in the outhouse, or if there were any Alpine spirits around, which she denied; she was very concerned that her house help would hear about the incident and would be terrified of staying alone when they travelled out of the city.

In Swiss folklore, the Alps have been known to be inhabited by mountain spirits like the Berggeist or the Alpine spirit, the Alpgeist, and there is many a tale about the Wild Hunt, a procession of ghostly hunters who march through the forests and mountains of Switzerland.

Mountains are mostly remote and isolated, shrouded in mystery and magic, and many, like Mount Kailash in Tibet, are considered sacred. Mountain tribes in the Himalayas have countless legends and myths attached to specific regions, towns and temples, and the local deity often boasts of powers to heal or destroy.

In our travels across the mountains, we have traversed the mid-Himalayan ranges of Kumaon and Garhwal, the Kangra and Sangla valleys in Himachal, and the higher Himalayas with their breathtaking views and idyllic villages where winter temperatures plummet to minus 35 degrees Celsius. On this particular occasion, we had travelled up to Khardung La, the highest pass in Leh–Ladakh, and the Pangong lake with its cotton wool clouds, startling blue waters, stark desert landscapes and indigo skies, dripping diamonds.

The ride to Pangong in 2008 was epic, with our colleagues from Teamwork, Ankur and Gilles Chuyen, consuming most of the oxygen from the portable cylinders as we ascended the mountain pass at 17,688 feet. Having had our fill of the spectacular view, the magnificent peaks in shades of brown contrasted against the peacock blue of the lake, we headed back, mindful of the fact that we were quite late and night would set in rapidly. Gilles was looking distinctly ill and needed to be taken back to Leh, which was located at a lower altitude. We had just crossed Khardung La when the driver accelerated and hurtled forward as he had noticed an avalanche racing down the slopes towards us. Seconds later, rock and snow crashed down and obliterated the road behind us. Thanking our stars, we drove on, only to be stopped by another landslide which had blocked the road ahead. As luck would have it, we were stuck behind an army convoy, and the men immediately swung into action and rescued Gilles, along with Ankur and Sheuli who had also begun feeling unwell. All three of them were suffering from high-altitude sickness and were evacuated to the army base camp and administered oxygen and medication.

When we had arrived in Leh for the company off-site, we had been advised complete bed rest for a day or two and given copious amounts of tea made of yak butter, which was horrid to drink but was supposed to help with altitude sickness. Given our penchant for adventure, we didn't stay in bed and traipsed off to a monastery and climbed up to a stupa before wandering around in the local market and, consequently, landed up with the most fearsome of all headaches. It was so bad that I wanted to chop my head off or take the next flight back. I called Puneeta and told her to cancel her flight as I was sure she wouldn't be able to cope with the high altitude.

Once the drama of our colleagues being rescued had died down and the army convoy had left for base camp, the rest of us made ourselves comfortable in the bus, settling down for what seemed likely to be a long night before the road was cleared and we could return to Leh.

The light from the full moon reflected off the whitened landscape. A sky full of stars forming the Milky Way, with not a tree in sight, convinced me that this was no accident and that we had been stranded there for a higher reason—perhaps an encounter with the mythical Yeti, the 'abominable snowman' believed to inhabit the higher Himalayas; or the elusive snow leopard whose habitation we were in.

Ladakh is known for its ghosts and spirits, from the red-skinned Lhande, who wander through the villages at night and cause illness, and whom you can encounter on a road at night, to the Tsan or the Bhut who lurk about, frightening unsuspecting travellers. Most Ladakhi houses tend to have an ochre stone placed at the threshold to ward off these spirits and keep their family and livestock safe.

In great anticipation of spotting either a mythical or mystical being, I tramped up the mountainside, much to the horror of Debaraj Mohanty who insisted we stay safe inside the bus. A meteor shower lit up the night sky as the shooting stars burnt a trail of iridescent light on entering the earth's atmosphere. As I slowly made my way uphill through the snow, I could see the bus appearing as a tiny speck of yellow light a little distance away. Having crested the hill, with nothing else in sight but the stars above and the ever-expanding white landscape all around, I decided to stop and take in the enormity of the universe and marvel at our own insignificance. Sadly, there was to be no Yeti nor snow leopard, Bhut or Lhande to be spotted, but what stayed with me was the expanse of the universe and the multitude of stars that surrounded us, truly a magnificent sight to behold and an image imprinted forever in my mind.

10

Spooked

Neemrana, Ramgarh, Ranikhet

The door creaked open and a beam of light cut through the staircase leading down to the basement. Our imaginations had conjured up skinned bodies hanging from hooks, salted and left to dry for days. The long worn wooden steps creaked as an apparition, covered from head to toe in hair, emerged … more bear than man! The sight was enough to chill our bones and send us straight back into the morning light.

One of the advantages of living in Delhi was that it's a few hours' drive from the mountains in the north and Rajasthan to the west, allowing for frequent getaways whenever the opportunity arose. I loved tearing up the roads with the kids in tow, car boot filled with enough food to feed an army, with the obligatory tins of spam and sardines, a variety of cheeses and cured meats, savouries and chocolates, and packets of Maggi noodles should there be an emergency or if we ran out of provisions for our ever-hungry kids.

For years, the Roys and Tejpals had holidayed together as often as possible. We counted down the days to the kids' summer, spring, winter and autumn breaks so we could plan our next getaway to savour the magic of Goa, the beauty of the Himalayas or the majesty and romance of Rajasthan. Tiya, Aditya, Cara and Avik were about the same age and studied at the Vasant Valley School which had been set up by Rekha and Aroon Purie and was run by new-age educationist Arun Kapoor, who envisioned holistic learning with a difference. Being liberal leftovers from the flower power generation, we had chosen Vasant Valley over the more traditional St. Columba's, Modern or Delhi Public School, staid institutions that somewhat accidentally educated the elite sent to their care.

Given our frenetic schedules, we were usually the last parents to arrive at the school for the annual or sports day functions and invariably landed up on the terrace as that was the only place empty, peering over the parapet, hoping to catch sight of the kids dressed up as a tree or a dinosaur or whatever the theme of the evening was, and feel redeemed. Tarun, Geetan and Puneeta and I had instantly struck up a friendship. We all lived in Safdarjung Enclave and the moms often met at birthday parties and while shepherding the kids to and from playdates in between their own work commitments. Tarun had just joined *India Today* after a stint with *The Indian Express* in Chandigarh, where he and Geetan had met in college and later worked together.

We were young parents, had much in common and were enthusiastic about tackling many of society's myriad problems. Long vodka-soaked evenings with a last-minute mad dash to the closest restaurant just as it was about to pull its shutters down, or dancing the night away at Bali Hi, the rooftop restaurant at ITC Maurya, or schlepping it to Fireball at 32nd Milestone marked our many outings laced with adventure and a bushelful of stories which we regaled our friends with.

When Tarun and Geetan moved out from Safdarjung to a new home in Soami Nagar, that became our party central for the next decade or so. Their home and hearts were always open, and they welcomed family and friends who streamed through each day, devouring innumerable butter-splattered parathas and copious amounts of aloo bhindi along with heaps of mutton, fish and chicken tikka kebabs.

Tarun's birthday is on 15 March, a day before mine, and in 2005, Holi and our birthdays lined up one after the other. The partying was monumental. Holi meant that anyone who dared to come to the house was first attacked with eggs, then rolled in a mud pit and splattered with colour, at which point the kids took over and drenched them with their pichkaris (squirt guns). The next day, we continued to party and set up a competition to see who could throw dough at the ceiling and make it stick. Many attempts later, there were several uncooked rotis stuck fast to the ceiling. (That summer, when the temperatures hit 42 degrees Celsius, the now cooked chapatis rained down on the guests below.) On the last night of this mad celebration, Gina (Annie Mathews) decided to help clean up after having consumed at least a full bottle of rum. She picked up a tray full of empty glasses and tripped, and we watched the tray fly out of her hand, wine and whiskey glasses smashing on the floor, in a scene straight out of a Peter Sellers film.

Our first autumn getaway in 1993 was to the Neemrana Fort located 110 km from Delhi. Prithviraj Chauhan III had won the fort from a local chieftain, Nimola Meva, and set up his capital there. In 1947, the ruling family, unable to look after the crumbling property, moved into smaller premises in the village below. In the mid-1980s, Aman Nath, Lekha Poddar and O.P. Jain, who were passionate about the arts, heritage and culture, bought the ruin from Chauhan's descendants and set about restoring it. Once Francis Wacziarg, a banker by profession, joined Aman in his effort to restore heritage properties, they began working on creating the iconic Neemrana Fort Hotels and Resorts, which grew to over twenty-seven heritage properties at the height of their success.

At the end of a two-hour drive from Delhi to the Rajasthan border, you turned off the highway and drove through the narrow winding village streets, navigating around uprooted stone slabs, changing to first gear as you revved the car up a steep incline that led to the fort entrance. Once there, you were instantly transported into the past.

A short walk past Chandni and Surya Mahal brought you to the main reception with an antique desk and newly upholstered chairs. The fort had been built across many levels running up the hill, with keekar trees and shrubs covering the hillside. At night, as you sat in its many courtyards looking out into the darkness, not a light could be seen for miles. An early winter chill made you reach for your shawl, even as the frost slowly settled over the mustard fields below.

Having put the kids to sleep, Tarun, Geetan, Puneeta and I gathered at the Malabar Suite, a vast room, quaintly done up with Rajasthani block print curtains, warm rugs, lamps, antique furniture and four-poster beds large enough to sleep a tribe. The bathroom was connected through a dimly lit corridor next to the suite's entrance. It was past midnight, and the hotel staff had long gone to sleep. Our friend and former TAG sound engineer Bapu, his wife Ajita, and Teamwork co-founder Mohit who had accompanied us on the trip had all headed to bed. The four of us were sipping vodka and chatting, recounting our experiences with ghosts, spirits and otherworldly beings. We were sitting with our backs to the suite's entrance when we heard a knock and then the door creaked open. We shouted for whoever it was to come in, but there was silence. Tarun got up to shut the door, assuming the wind had blown it open, only to realize that the heavy antique doors opened outwards and that the wind could not have blown them open. Peering out into the cool night, he couldn't see anyone in the courtyard, the corridor or the passage to the bathrooms. A slow realization that this could well be a spirit sank in, and Geetan and Puneeta, totally spooked, refused to go to the loo without one of us standing guard at the entrance to the corridor. Our own suite was some distance away and we decided to walk back as a group.

Weeks later, we met up with Aman and Francis and enquired if the fort was haunted and if there had been any sightings in the past. They flatly denied that they had ever encountered a spook before.

At our next holiday, we took a road trip to Ranikhet; we had planned a night's halt at Talla Ramgarh, before heading out to Binsar National Park, driving on from there to Ranikhet before returning to Delhi. We stopped at Kiran and Bidi's house at Talla Ramgarh. Once evening fell, a fire was lit and bottles of rum were opened. Bidi began regaling us with stories of their ancestral palaces and the ghosts that had inhabited them. Both husband and wife were from erstwhile royal families with palaces in Nainital and Kumaon. As the evening progressed and more quarter bottles of rum were sent for, Bidi mentioned that at the cottage we were to stay in, there was a resident ghost the size of a large Himalayan bear, black as the night, who walked up and down the property and leapt upon unsuspecting guests and twisted their necks straight off. Certainly not the most comforting way to welcome guests or wrap up a night in a strange place!

He offered to move our luggage from the guest house into the main building. We were now convinced that what they really wanted to do was murder us at night, skin us and smoke us to perfection! We refused to move, collected the kids and headed back to the guest house, only to find that it was totally flooded. We had to search around for bricks to lay down on the floor so that we could cross to the bathroom. Despite the mess, however, we decided that we would all sleep in one room with the kids and deal with any ghost or ghoul together if it appeared.

Early the next morning, as the sun emerged and lit up the great Himalayan peaks, we headed for breakfast to the main house and as we settled in to eat the fruits laid out, this apparition appeared covered in fur, more bear than man—it was in fact Bidi, who slept with their many dogs and was covered in their hair. We gathered the kids and our belongings, bid goodbye to our hosts and set off for the Binsar wildlife sanctuary where we were to spend a night before driving on to Ranikhet.

The hill station of Ranikhet was established in 1869 as a military cantonment in Almora district which allowed the British forces to control the warring hill states in the region. The panoramic views of the Himalayan peaks make it a much-loved destination for tourists who head there for their summer holidays.

The Westview Hotel, which was to be our home for the next few days, was built in 1918 in the colonial architectural style with old-world stone and wood, and echoed its colonial past with afternoon tea being served with freshly baked scones, clotted cream and strawberry jam.

We unpacked and ordered up mounds of French fries and kebabs, strawberry milkshakes and chilli chicken and settled in for the night, swapping stories and regaling our old friend Seema Rao and her daughters, Aditi and Alisha, who had joined us on this leg of our holiday. We invariably got around to recounting stories about some of the spirits and ghosts we had encountered. As the night grew long and the wind picked up outside, rattling the doors and windows, we realized that we had managed to spook ourselves with our own stories! Seema and her daughters refused to walk back to their cottage alone. Tarun and I escorted them back and ensured them that there were no ghouls or monsters hiding under the bed or in the closet. On our way back, we considered pulling a prank and throwing a pebble at their window, but knew that if we had done so, Seema would probably have had a heart attack in sheer fright.

Back at the cottage, Cara, Tarun and Geetan's younger daughter, suddenly sat bolt upright, shrieking, her eyes glazed over, face expressionless. We were terrified. Her parents rushed over and held her close, asking her what had happened, what she had seen, if she was in pain, but Cara didn't respond; her eyes stayed glazed over till she slowly calmed down and went back to sleep. The next morning, she had no recollection of what had frightened her. We didn't know if it was a nightmare, an apparition, or the stories she had heard that had subconsciously triggered her fear.

11

Healing

Gurgaon

Not a leaf stirred; humidity hung heavy in the air. The traffic lights blinked nervously, amber on, amber off, alerting late-night drivers to slow down as they approached the intersection. But the speeding gypsy in front of us neither paused nor heeded the sign and hurtled through the crossing, hitting a scooter that had slowed down. The rider's helmet flew off as he was flung into the air and slammed onto the unyielding road, thick crimson blood oozing from his head as his life force ebbed out of him.

Puneeta and I were driving down Lodhi Road when the accident took place. The gypsy paused briefly, the driver leaning out of the window to see what had happened; at the sight of the crumpled body, he must have panicked. He sped off into the night. We stopped, called the cops and the emergency services who arrived soon after, sirens piercing the night, lights flashing. Yet, even as they transferred the body onto the stretcher, you could tell that the victim hadn't survived the accident. We looked at the ambulance pulling away into the distance with a sense of disquiet and sadness.

We drove back home in silence, thinking about the shock the victim's family would experience when they received news of the tragedy. As we crawled into bed, Puneeta sent the departed soul love, light and healing, and drifted off to sleep.

A few hours later, I woke up with a start and perceived a red energy towering above me, filled with anguish and rage. The victim of the accident had travelled back with us, disoriented and distraught. I apologized to him and explained that we had nothing to do with his death, that we had stopped to help him and had waited till the ambulance arrived, while the gypsy that hit him had sped off. Death from a sudden accident invariably leads to a great deal of confusion for the victim's spirit. It takes them time to understand that they no longer inhabit their body and they aren't quite sure how to respond and where to go. Many of us have unresolved issues when we die, especially if we die young and unexpectedly, and these need healing and closure. It took a while to calm him down as Puneeta sent him healing energy and guided him towards the light.

Puneeta had begun her journey in self-healing in September 1996 by exploring and learning Reiki, a holistic therapy based on the philosophy that a universal life force flows through all human beings. A Reiki practitioner develops the ability to channel this energy through their hands or via distant healing to the person in need, and it has been known to heal those with chronic pain and emotional challenges, and rebalance the body's energies. For a while, Puneeta and her colleague Urmila had worked actively with Gurudev to learn and assimilate healing practices which they channelled at the KRC. In 2000, Gurudev persuaded Sharupa, Dilip, Puneeta and me to take a Reiki course, which we did with grandmaster Adarsh Puri who initiated us into the practice; as Gurudev later said, it helped adjust my antenna and hone my ability to receive messages from the universe.

Many of these changes coincided with our move from Delhi to our new home in Gurgaon, which, in 1997, seemed to be at the end of the world. Pa asked Puneeta to accompany him to sus out a plot of land that had been allocated to him by the Haryana government in Sector 15, fairly close to Fireball. You had to drive through Mehrauli on a two-lane road till you reached Garden Estate, where you could stop at the wonderful Village Shop and buy organic vegetables, cakes, jams and quiches, and then continue down the Delhi–Jaipur highway to the 32nd Milestone complex where many a night was spent drinking and dancing.

Puneeta came away totally in love with the plot of land she had seen and persuaded us to consider building a new home there, away from the centre of Delhi. Opposite our plot, there was a green belt which had a mini golf course, tennis courts and a rose garden, and she felt this was ideal for the kids to play, ride a bike and breathe fresh air in. (All of these seemed overrated to me and I saw the move as a major distraction from our busy social life and our easy access to evening entertainment and our friends.)

My father called up a few of his friends and asked them to recommend a builder. A 'fine fellow' who hailed from General Shankar Roy Choudhary's regiment had recently set up a construction firm and was keen to take on the project. The good colonel drew up architectural plans and included our varied suggestions: large master bedrooms with walk-in closets, a spacious kitchen, storage areas, a loo for guests, and the location of Ma's puja room according to the principles of Vaastu.

Having finalized the plans and given the builder an advance, we collectively forget all about the house.

A year or so later when I did remember that we had a building project underway, we decided to set out to see what progress had been made. Apart from a brand-new Mercedes car, the good colonel had precious little to show building-wise. The foundation, some pillars and the casing of the ground-floor roof were in place, but the roof itself was yet to be cast. Calls were made to the general who had recommended the 'fine fellow', who, in turn, was spoken with and commanded to make good his commitment. The colonel, very much in the 'khate, peete, changa (eat, drink, enjoy)' mould, demurred and demanded more money before he proceeded any further. The building process continued in fits and starts, mostly due to our continued neglect and our reluctance to drive out to see what was being done regularly.

I had been caught up in keeping Teamwork afloat, which was close to bankruptcy since we had stopped most of our television work. Our plan of creating a sustainable performing arts platform was yet to be realized. While Friends of Music, set up by Mohit, Kanika and Val, was a club for emerging new music—not quite pop or rock or Bollywood, but something much more homegrown, like Indian Ocean, Mrigya, Silk Route, Parikrama and Orange Street, who played at monthly concerts, bringing together music lovers and people from the world of advertising, academia and business—we still had a long way to go in making any of this pay for itself.

I had begun some advisory work with the British Council and was part of their arts management faculty, which took me to the annual Edinburgh Festival, the largest in the world; it was not just awe-inspiring and jaw-dropping, but it also allowed us to build a network with arts venues and presenters from across the world. While the sheer scale of what you got to see at the festival was impressive, I found the lack of work featured from India puzzling. Determined to make the most of the visit, Puneeta and I marched from show to show, criss-crossing Edinburgh as the venues were spread far apart, rationing what we ate or drank to save money. I had budgeted three pounds per meal for both of us and that included beverages for the day. What this meant was lining up at the hot potato shop on Market Street and sharing a fully loaded jacket potato with cheese, cream, bacon and pickles, or buying a sandwich from Tesco, a supermarket. One day, fed up with the rationing, Puneeta demanded her own full jacket potato, a bottle of water and a packet of biscuits—pure luxury. As it happened, the server picked out the largest potato and loaded it with all the toppings, which she then struggled to finish, even as I glowered at her for breaking the bank.

The Edinburgh Festivals are a conglomeration of six arts platforms including the Festival Fringe, the

Royal Military Tattoo, the Edinburgh International Book Festival, the Film Festival and the Art Festival. The oldest of these is the Edinburgh International Festival, which was set up in 1947, after World War II, as a way to bring new resources to a very impoverished and war-impacted region. The International Festival hosted an array of theatre, Western classical music and opera productions in the city's principal venues and was funded by the government. Eight theatre groups that had not been invited to the main festival took over smaller, alternative venues and were labelled 'festival adjuncts' or the semi-official festival. A critic did review these productions, referring to them as being on the 'fringe of the official festival', and the name stuck. In 1948, Robert Kemp, a playwright, opined that indeed 'round the fringe of official festival drama, there seemed to be more private enterprise than before'. Since then, the Fringe Festival has used every possible alternative site, including repurposed heritage churches, community centres, basements and street corners, toilets and lifts. Alongside this profusion of theatre was born the Edinburgh International Book Festival that was first held at the iconic Lighthouse Bookshop on Nicholson Street, and to that was added the Edinburgh Film Festival, the Jazz Festival, a TV conference for professionals, and the spectacular Edinburgh Tattoo, organized on the ramparts of the Edinburgh Castle, with a coming together of the consolidated bands of the Pipes and Drums.

Back in India, realizing that the building project in Gurgaon was not going to be completed without us actually moving in there, we bid goodbye to our Safdarjung Enclave home of thirteen years, packed with memories of ghosts and ghouls, visiting spirits and our many friends and colleagues who had partied on the rooftop, including Shah Rukh and Gauri, who had been dating for a while and had decided to get married and had filed for permission to do so in a civil court. As a primary witness to the court marriage, I had given our home address on the legal form. The local Vishwa Hindu Parishad (VHP) functionaries arrived just before the pre-wedding sangeet that we were hosting at home began, banging degchis (large empty vessels) in protest and demanding that the inter-religious wedding be called off. Pa, as a senior fauji, went down and read them the riot act, after which they backed off reluctantly. This, sadly, was a harbinger of what was to happen across north India in the following decades.

There were other celebrations in the Safdarjung Enclave house—actor Rituraj and Charu's wedding, and a historic dinner that we hosted with Zohra Sehgal and Uzra Appa, sisters from across the border who were reunited after fifty years through the play *Ek Thi Nani*. And the many themed parties, including an effort to recreate Goa in Delhi by laying out mounds of sand on the terrace.

We bid adieu to the peepul tree outside our bedroom window with its lost souls, the headless warriors who inhabited Puneeta's office area, our landlords and neighbours, the familiarity of INA and Khan Market, the Green Chick Chop store which had supplied us with endless amounts of kebabs and other savouries, and set out for our new home. We all moved into the ground floor and asked the workers to leave, after which it took another few years and two more contractors before we were able to complete the house and move upstairs with Iram Sultan Mukherjee's considered advice on colours and tiling, stone patterns and upholstery weaves. Iram would go on to become the most sought-after interior designer, with a wonderful aesthetic sense of colour and form, designing the Zydus Cadila Office, and many farmhouses and projects for DLF.

A new house comes with its own energies. Ma, a great believer in Durga and Kali, had Mukul da, the head priest at Matri Mandir in Safdarjung Enclave, our go-to temple during Durga Puja and on other important occasions, perform a havan and consecrate the house. When we first began construction, Mukul da had presided over the ground-breaking ceremony, consigning a silver snake, a gold coin and a copper plate to Mother Earth, embedding these in the foundation stone in an auspicious part of the property, along with donations of grains and ghee, sweets and clothes to propitiate the navagrahas (nine planets) and the presiding gods, and requesting them to bless us and our home with good energy, good health and good fortune.

The first floor, with its wraparound balcony through which the sun streamed in, was lovely and looked out on to the green belt and the peepul and banyan trees we had planted. We found space for our vast collection of art and memorabilia accumulated over the years from our travels across the world: masks from Venice, Florence and the National Theatre in London; auspicious Chinese lion figurines acquired from Singapore, juxtaposed against blue Spode; Greek, Turkish and Egyptian plates mounted on either side of an antique mirror inherited from my mother's home in Calcutta; a statue of a monk which had been carried back by Aditya from our holiday in Krabi—each object carefully chosen and transported over long distances, with a story of its own. The formal living areas were separated by a foyer, and a corridor lined with bookshelves opened up to our bedrooms, which, in turn, overlooked the back garden.

Our bedroom had parquet flooring, a purple and white distressed wall and a king-sized wrought-iron bed flanked by side tables that overflowed with a clutch of homoeopathy medicines, and two stunning photographs, including the Dome of the Rock and the Wailing Wall, that Mohit had taken when he was in Jerusalem and gifted to us at our wedding. Our bed was large enough to accommodate all four of us and the resident animals when required. Aditya and Avik often crawled into our bed at night, spooked either by a sound or a presence they felt in their room. Aditya often referred to a lady with a distinct perfume who came and perched herself at the foot of their bed, freaking them out. He used to snuggle up next to Puneeta, while Avik would nudge me till I rolled over to one side and then crawl in, inevitably leading to a battle for the razai, with each side pulling the quilt off the other.

One night, following a late dinner and some very good red wine which had put us in a fairly mellow mood, Puneeta and I went to bed all set for what I hoped would be a lovely long sleep—only to be nudged awake by Avik who was trying to get me to move so he could climb into our bed. Puneeta shouted at us to settle down after the unavoidable battle for the quilt and a few attempts to smack each other with pillows over her head, more to annoy her than anything else.

Suddenly, Avik paused, and in his deep baritone voice, which he brings on when serious, said, 'Papa, yaar, what the f..k, what's that on the ceiling?' I looked up to see a red orb- or ectoplasm-like thing hovering about near the fan. In no mood to deal with an annoying ghost, I mumbled that it was nothing and we should sleep.

A second later, Avik said, 'Papa, yaar, what the f..k, it's not moving … it's just there.' I told him it was probably the reflection of the red light from a passing ambulance (which was impossible, given that our bedroom was recessed from the main road). Avik refused to settle down till I got out of bed, put on the light and generally asked whatever it was to bugger off—and told Puneeta to send it much light and ask it to go back to wherever it had come from. Luckily, whatever Puneeta did helped, and the orb moved on and we all went back to sleep.

12

Narrow Escapes

New York, Bali, Boulder

In 2022, I was headed to America on an exploratory visit to see if we could expand our festival footprint to the New World. Mira Nair, a dear friend and award-winning film director, had offered to host me at her home for a few nights while I was in New York. Mira had told me she would be back home by 10 p.m. and that suited me well. After clearing the interminable Homeland Security lines at JFK Airport, I took the A-train from Howard Junction, and hoped to alight at the subway station closest to Riverside Drive on the Upper West Side and then walk from there. The cab fare of sixty-five dollars from the airport to the city felt steep and this seemed to be a way more affordable option to get me there on time.

Those were still the early years of our transition from being a film- and TV-content producing company to an arts organization, and money and resources were scarce at best. It took a fair amount of effort and preparation to tap into our existing networks to see if there was any interest in hosting a platform for the performing and visual arts from India, which weren't as fashionable then as they are now, two and a half decades later. The diaspora was yet to emerge from its primary concerns of roti, kapda aur makaan (food, clothing and shelter) and become a confident community comfortable in its identity and proud of its tradition and culture. Mainstream venues in major cities, especially in New York, were still recovering from the impact of 9/11 and were suspicious of foreigners. We had just begun establishing international platforms for the arts from India, with Shweta Asnani moving to Singapore in 2000 to set up a branch of Teamwork and to leverage the investment that the city state had made into its arts infrastructure. Soon after, Lakshmi Laroia headed to Hong Kong; having been at the helm of ZEE TV programming in its inception years, she was keen to get back to creating new work in films and the arts. Given our recent success at the Festivals Edinburgh, where we had created a platform for exceptional contemporary and classical work from India, it seemed that this was the time to explore new opportunities across the world and look both East and West.

New York's subway system is not for the faint-hearted. The fumes of stale urine suspended in gassy tunnels, spooks frightened out of in-between spaces by rattling trains and clattering tiles, the collective gloom of failure, mental illness and despair in Gothamesque proportions—they could drive you straight out to the grimy neon-lit streets of post-9/11 New York!

I gathered my laptop-laden rucksack and wheelie, stepped on board an A-train and settled in for a spot of people-watching. New Yorkers are fascinating: the fashion of the day; hues of grey and black, topped with purple, green and pink; masses of curls and bald pates, clashing with spikes and steel pierced through human flesh; the patched coats of the homeless people and the bag ladies, their hopes squeezed into sleeping bags, breathing in the pain of crumpled dreams, trying to fight off the damp and the cold creeping up their torn stockings. You invariably wondered about their lives: young lust, testosterone driven, fuelled by the intoxicant of the day; mothers cocooned with their children, nurturing their dreams, watching time; executives caught up in their busyness; and so many with no place to go, staring out into the vacantness of their subterranean refuge, their lives flashing by as they travelled through grime-coated tunnels to unknown endings.

As we sped past 86th Street, I realized I was on an express train that had limited stops on the A-line and it wouldn't stop at the station where I wanted to get off to go to Riverside Drive. I got off at the 125th Street station and in trying to find a way to cross platforms and head back on a returning all-stops train, somehow found myself at the subway exit. It was well past 9 p.m. when I stepped out onto the street; a cold wind picked up bits of paper, making them somersault in the air and then burying them in the mounds of trash on the sidewalks. It took me a while to orient myself to my immediate surroundings, only to realize that I was in the heart of what I presumed to be Harlem, with boarded-up shop windows and shuttered homes, and chinks of light slicing the pavement into no-go zones. Rather than look for a street map, I decided to follow my instinct and walk up the street, hoping I was headed in the direction of Riverside Drive.

Hurried footsteps behind me alerted me to possible danger. I glanced into a window and saw the silhouette of two men in hoodies match their steps to mine. At the corner, sensing that they were about to rush me, I turned around and asked them for directions to Columbia University, hoping my salt-and-pepper hair would rouse their sympathy and they wouldn't mug me.

The men stopped in their tracks, startled, looked at each other and indicated that I should continue to walk up the street. There wasn't much I could do; those were pre-Google map days and there wasn't a soul on the street or even an open shop to seek refuge in. The wind picked up; a slash of light split the sidewalk as someone parted their curtains to look out and hastily drew them again before I could gesture for help. In an opaque dust-laden shop window, I noticed one of the men reach into his waistband and draw something out. Was it a gun, a knife? I had no way of knowing. With a growing sense of panic, I hurried without seeming to, pacing my steps so as to not give them any reason to rush. They matched me, step to step; when I increased my pace, they did too; when I stopped to adjust the strap of my knapsack, they paused; when I passed my roll-on from one hand to the other, they skipped a step, but stayed just a few feet behind me, their shadows menacing, their presence overpowering.

The pedestrian light at the crossing had turned green and even as I hastened to cross the street, a yellow cab hurtled down the road and screeched to a halt in front of me. The driver threw open the door, shouted at me to jump in and the second I got in, he floored the accelerator, jumped the light and sped away. I glanced back at the two men. They stood there, weapon in hand, arguing with each other and showing the cabbie the finger.

The warmth of the cab was a relief. The turbaned Sikh driver launched into a tirade and wanted to know what I was doing in the middle of the night in the heart of Harlem; did I not realize that the men following me were armed and would have robbed me at gunpoint and possibly shot me if I had resisted? When I thanked him in Hindi for coming to my rescue, he seemed surprised that I was Indian—he had thought I was from South America. He proceeded to lecture me on how unsafe New York was, especially those areas. He then asked about India and where my home was and shared his stories and experiences with guns and violence in a city which had seen it all.

To this day, I have no idea what the cab driver himself was doing in Harlem at night and how he had realized I was in trouble and needed rescuing. As I sank into the sofa at Mira and Mahmoud's lovely Riverside Drive apartment with a glass of good red wine, I could only thank the universe and my guides or angels for watching out for me.

Some months later, I flew to Indonesia to meet Ambassador Shyam Saran who had been recently posted there and was keen to set up a festival to celebrate the age-old connections of commerce, trade, culture, religion and heritage between the two countries. He had reached out to us at Teamwork Films, as we were known then, and we had begun exploring the possibilities of creating a three-week extravaganza of dance, music, theatre, food, fashion and visual arts in each of the major Indonesian cities including Borobudur, Bandung, Jog Jakarta, Jakarta and Bali. Megawati Sukarnoputri was the then president and she loved Bollywood; the plan was to stage a mega show starring Shah Rukh Khan, Rani Mukherjee and the just-emerging actress Priyanka Chopra. We had tied up with an Indonesian broadcaster, who was also a primary sponsor for the festival, to beam the show across Indonesia.

Setting up a festival in any foreign country is always a challenge as well as an adventure, and Indonesia, steeped in traditions and a culture akin to ours, had the added charm of its own myriad art forms, including Wayang, a shadow puppet tradition used to tell stories from the Ramayana and the Mahabharata; Gamelan music, with its complex cymbals and bells that accompanied the Wayang performances; and the vibrant textile tradition of double-ikat, which was used to clothe the wooden puppet characters in these performances along with magnificent masks and head gears.

Over centuries, many cultural forms and stories from India had travelled east from the coast of Orissa, Andhra Pradesh and Tamil Nadu on trading ships carrying cotton, silk and gold, along with philosophy, cultural traditions and religious practices, which, over time, had been adapted by the local inhabitants.

On the way to Borobudur and its famed temple, you could stop at any roadside shack and eat a chicken ayam, tender whole or cut chicken marinated in local spices and then tossed in light flour and fried, served up with the most delectable sauce made of garlic, ginger, coriander and chillies, which certainly rates amongst the best chicken dishes I have ever tasted.

Jakarta, with its snarled traffic, was a city where scooter taxis made more sense than air-conditioned limousines to help weave through the chaotic streets. The cheek-by-jowl housing and the constantly overflowing roads and lanes converged at main artery points which were invariably blocked, and no number of flyovers could help ease the flow of traffic. If you were heading out to a meeting or an official dinner, you had no way of knowing if you would be late, reach on time or arrive an hour early (in which case, the host and the hostess indulged you while getting rid of their hair curlers and changing out of their sweatpants). In contrast to the hurly-burly of the city, the houses of the wealthy were oases of peace and calm, with streams of water cascading over carved stone and flowing into extravagant blue-tiled swimming pools.

Bali was a total contrast to Jakarta. Its quaint international airport, designed and decorated in the traditional architectural style, immediately transported you into a different world. The muggy heat of an overcrowded city fell away as you walked through the airport, cool air blowing through the open corridors framed by carved wooden pillars in adherence to local traditions, where the most sacred spaces are built facing in the direction of the mountains, believed to be the abode of the gods and their ancestors, and the relatively unclean spaces face the sea, supposedly inhabited by demons who bring about tsunamis and steal away unsuspecting people who have stepped into it.

Over 90 per cent of the Balinese population follows a form of Hinduism or Buddhism whose origins can be traced back to the first century CE. The people believe that the gods and goddesses are present in every form of nature and in the produce of nature, be it rivers, trees, plants, rocks or everyday objects like woven fabric, knives and bowls. Given the highly ritualistic traditions in self-discipline and movement, they have evolved intricate and sophisticated art forms, including painting, and you'll find visual art, woodcarving, handicrafts and performance styles which portray stories from Hindu epics.

Our host, the governor of Bali, had instructed his ADC to be our minder during the recce. The ADC, who introduced himself as a Brahmin from Haryana, was seen as a person of eminence on the island, given his caste and origins. He whisked us off to the Bali Beach Hotel, built by President Sukarno in the early 1960s and refurbished thereafter; the hotel sat on 42 acres of land right on the white sand beaches of Sanur. Having deposited our luggage and freshened up, we set off to explore possible venues in Ubud, the cultural hub of the island located up in the hills, north of its capital city, Denpasar.

Ubud is a charming hill resort with its streets lined with painters and wood carvers producing the most intricate work on teak, mahogany, sonokeling or the popular jati wood. The hotels and spas are beautifully appointed, with white gossamer fabric separating massage areas, restaurants and table settings, and offering panoramic views of magnificent sunrises or sunsets depending on the orientation of the space, be it to the east or the west. The dappled pools of the Half Moon restaurant reflected the overhanging banyan trees and coconut groves, and the aromas of hibiscus, jasmine and frangipani mingled with that of the delicately scented incense sticks that greeted you at every point created a heady mix. The table seating recessed at the end of the pools of water reflected the moon on most nights and was ideal for music concerts or poetry and book readings. Years later, the restaurant would become the venue for the annual Ubud Literature Festival, which is a must-visit for writers from across the world.

Having spent the day exploring all that nature had to offer and sampling the exquisitely balanced Balinese food, we headed to Kuta to experience its numerous nightclubs and restaurants which made it the most popular tourist destination in Bali. The ADC had instructed the driver to drop us to Kuta on our way back—but this was perhaps lost in translation, for the driver headed straight back to our hotel in Denpasar. Having reached there, we decided to freshen up and then set out for Kuta in a cab ordered from the hotel. As we drove through Denpasar, every roadside café and restaurant beckoned with mouthwatering displays of suckling pig and roast duck hung in their windows. We decided to savour some of these fabled dishes and asked the driver to drop us off and told him that we would hail a local cab and continue to Kuta post dinner.

The Balinese way of roasting pork is considered an art form. The pig is marinated in turmeric, garlic, shallots, ginger, lemongrass, galangal, coriander seeds, chillies, kaffir lime leaves and salam leaves, then grilled over a wooden spit or gas fire till it gives up its juices and is roasted to golden perfection. The fat dripping, the flesh tender and the skin firm and crisp, you dip it in an array of sauces and accompaniments and experience food heaven. Bali, being a Hindu kingdom, is the only place in Indonesia where you can find pork on offer at restaurants.

Having eaten way more than we should have and washed it down with some Balinese beer, which was less exciting than the local rice brew that's fermented in every household and sold off the tap, we decided to set off for Kuta. It was 10.30 p.m. by the time we left the restaurant, and I was conscious of the fact that I had a 6 a.m. flight the next morning and would have to leave the hotel no later than 4.30 a.m.

We hailed two mobike cabs whom we haggled with till they agreed to what we thought was an acceptable price. The drivers protested loudly that in Bali no one negotiated as cheating a guest was considered a sin. The wind blowing through our hair, a song on our lips, we sped past rice fields … until, suddenly, the drivers pulled over by the roadside and asked us for more money, without which they refused to go any further—so much for accumulating sin and cheating tourists. Annoyed, we got off the bikes, asked where we were and, realizing that we weren't far from our hotel, abandoned our plans to go to Kuta and headed back to our rooms to catch some sleep before flying out the next morning.

I hate early morning flights and this was no exception. Bleary-eyed and cranky, I set off for the local airport to catch a flight to Bandung and from there on to Melbourne to audition dancers for the upcoming Commonwealth Games Arts Festival which I had been asked to direct. The airport was deserted;

the security guard was busy singing and dancing to a Bollywood song and joyfully waved me through without the mandatory pat down. As I sat waiting for the flight, I scrolled through my phone and saw a number of missed calls from Puneeta. I immediately called her back, wondering what may have happened. She was frantic and asked where I had been, why I hadn't been taking her calls and if I had gone to Kuta. She said she had been trying to reach me at the hotel and on my mobile but hadn't been able to do so. Then she asked if I had heard about the bomb blast in Bali and described the visuals that had been streaming across news channels. I told her not to believe what she saw on TV as the media wasn't to be trusted and that absolutely nothing had happened; while we had never made it to Kuta beach, there wasn't any news of an untoward incident, let alone a terror attack. It was only when I landed in Bandung and was received there by my colleagues and the embassy representatives that I learned about the horrific terror attack.

The previous night, at about 11 p.m., there were three bomb blasts, two in Kuta and one at the American consulate in Denpasar. A total of 202 people were killed and countless others injured on that busy Saturday night when the bars and clubs were packed with tourists and locals. A suicide bomber had walked into the popular Paddy's Bar and set off the first bomb, while a van parked outside the Sari Club was remotely detonated. The force of the blasts was so great that the glass windows of every restaurant within a one-mile radius were shattered. The Balinese, a gentle and courteous people who lived in accordance with their traditions of civility and were accustomed to an unhurried, peaceful way of life, were stunned. Thirty-nine Indonesians were among those killed that night in the blasts. Later, the Jemaah Islamiyah, a Southeast Asian Jihadist organization linked to the al-Qaeda, claimed responsibility for the attack. For us, this had been a narrow escape; thrice we had set out for Kuta, and thrice we had been thwarted by some invisible force and protected from harm.

A decade or so later, in 2013, having successfully established the Jaipur Literature Festival with Namita Gokhale and William Dalrymple as our festival co-directors, we had grown in size, stature and reputation and were exploring the possibility of setting up the first edition of the JLF in USA. JLF London had been our first international edition, and we were hoping to take some of that magic to America.

Earlier that year, three visitors to the festival in Jaipur had written an impassioned email to William Dalrymple detailing why we should consider Boulder, Colorado, as the natural home for the American edition.

Maruta Kanins, with her long flowing white hair, was a practising Buddhist from the flower power generation. She had lived in Nepal with her Tibetan translator partner, had brought up their children there and finally relocated to Boulder, where she set up a boutique store selling Indian jewellery embellished with precious and semi-precious stones, shawls, rugs, brass and copper statues and other objets d'art from the subcontinent. Maruta had been attending the Jaipur festival from its inception, and at one of the editions, she met Jessie Friedman, a psychologist, and Jules Levinson, a Tibetan translator, both residents of Boulder, who had accidently wandered into the festival on their way back from a conference in Sanchi where they had gone to listen to His Holiness the Dalai Lama. Bowled over by the breadth of the conversations and the range of topics on offer at the festival and the vibrant and energized audiences, the three of them were convinced that JLF had to come to Boulder.

Not being entirely sure where Boulder was, I checked it out on the map and determined that I would need to fly to Denver, which was the closest major airport, and hitch a ride out to this city at the base of the Flatirons, a distinctive rock formation that looked like the flat side of an iron, located at the foothills of the Rocky Mountains. Going in person to Boulder was the only way to determine if the audacious plan of hosting JLF in the middle of nowhere would work; so I headed there.

Maruta agreed to drive out 65 km to the airport and ferry me back to Boulder. Denver, also known as the Mile-High City, had startling blue skies, and its rolling fields were covered with snow in winter. As you headed out of the city, the highway rose and dipped till at one point you could see the entire stretch of the Flatirons spread across the horizon. A freak blizzard had just blown through the area and the roads were iced over; interestingly, over the next few years, each time I travelled to Boulder, I always met with a snowstorm or a blizzard.

Maruta's car had seen far better years and given that it was used to fetch her grandchildren and doubled as a pickup for her merchandise, it was the worse for wear. We were chatting and catching up on local gossip and she was sharing background details about our to-be local partners—Jessie Freidman and Jules Levinson—when three prairie dogs suddenly popped up on the road ahead. Given the icy conditions and the speed Maruta was driving at, it would have been madness to swerve, and yet, because of her deep Buddhist beliefs and compassion for all living things, she swerved! The rest unfolded in slow motion: I braced and told her not to slam the brakes, even as she did so. The tyres screeched, the car creaked and jackknifed, momentarily losing its grip on the road, and turned a full 180 degrees till it righted itself and came to a stop at the edge of the embankment, thankfully without flipping over.

It took a moment for us to collect ourselves and for the panic to ease, and as we looked around we saw that the traffic had pulled up on both sides of the expressway to avoid what could have been a nasty highway pile up. I let out a sigh of relief and joked with Maruta that the universe had protected us and that this was an omen, a sign to set up JLF in Boulder. Since then, JLF Colorado, held at the Boulder Public Library, has been our mothership event in the United States, with new editions emanating out of there to include Houston, New York, Seattle and North Carolina.

Before flying out to Denver, I was staying at The Public, a wonderful boutique hotel in Chicago, just off the Golden Mile and two blocks from the lake. A quaint clock whose hands moved backwards through time framed the reception desk, and lamps shaped like planets in the solar system hung from the ceiling in the dining hall, which boasted the best breakfast in the vicinity and doubled up as the sexiest nightclub in town. I returned to my room at night to find a bottle of champagne and a note from the hotel manager apologizing and asking me to call. Intrigued, I dialled the reception desk and was informed that a full-length wall mirror had shattered inexplicably during the day, covering the floor and the room in shards of broken glass which housekeeping had cleaned up. Given that I hadn't even noticed the missing mirror when I returned to my room, I thought nothing of it till the mishap the next morning in Denver.

Was it a 'totka', the breaking of a spell—a way of warding off impending evil, or was it sheer coincidence? What I do know is that there are angels who seem to be on hand to help protect me each time I head towards potential trouble.

13

The Ravages of History

Edinburgh

The cloud cover broke as the aircraft banked on its final descent and the rays from a freshly minted sun fell on the Forth Bridge over the Firth, and the verdant hills painted in watercolour hues of green, speckled with splashes of snowy white sheep and neatly bound bales of hay, appeared freshly washed. Scotland, a land of legends and valour, lochs and monsters, storms and cobbled stone, rain and fog, malt and whiskey, tartan and castles, was a world steeped in antiquity and tradition, waiting to be explored.

The year was 2002, and I was returning to Edinburgh, which had become a favourite city of sorts. From our very first visit in 1999, which was thanks to the ever-energetic Sushma Bahl, the legendary Director of Arts at British Council, India, who wanted me to experience the annual Edinburgh Festival which brought in artistes and performers, agents and festival directors from across the world, we fell deeply in love with the city, its people and the diversity and magnitude of the arts on display.

On that visit to the festival, Puneeta and I stayed at a B&B on Dalkeith Road, past the Commonwealth swimming pool, at thirty pounds a night. The British Council had arranged to pay for shows recommended by them or chosen by us, and each day we would wake up at 8.30 a.m., get dressed, take the bus to the city centre and be in our seats by 10 a.m. to catch the first performance of the day. Not being acquainted with the geography of the city, we had booked back-to-back shows in venues that were spread across Old and New Town. This had us walking at a brisk pace uphill and downhill, through meadows and alleyways connecting the two distinct parts of the city that were divided by the Princes Street Gardens, now a beautiful venue for public concerts and Sunday picnics but which in earlier times had been the moat that surrounded the Edinburgh Castle into which all refuse and human waste was dumped. Typically, we ended the day with a late-night stand-up comedy show that the Fringe Festival was known for, at the Assembly Rooms on George Street, recognized as being amongst the most prestigious venues at the Fringe, with an eclectic programme of cutting-edge theatre, sold-out comedy and the odd music performance which was curated and produced by the legendary arts entrepreneur, William 'Bill' Burdett-Coutts.

The Edinburgh Festival, with over 33,000 shows spread across a four-week period, is truly a melting pot of creativity and diversity, representing the arts from every part of the world. Performers in those days could apply for a tourist visa and travel to the festival, having booked a Fringe Festival venue to showcase their work. While there were hundreds of venues that hosted shows, the main stages of the Fringe Festival were the Traverse Theatre, the Assembly Rooms, the Pleasance, C-Venues and Aurora Nova, curated by Wolfgang Hoffmann, at St. Stephen's, a repurposed church.

Edinburgh is enigmatic, mysterious, historic and exists in the twilight between the past and the present. The Old Town was awarded UNESCO heritage city status in 1995, preserving its closes and historic buildings that flank the Edinburgh Castle and the Royal Mile. The buildings exist at many different levels, often going down seven floors deep to the bedrock below street level. These were used as living quarters by families that had escaped the Irish potato famine and by the servants who served the rich merchants, royal courtiers, lords and ladies of the capital city.

Back in the day, it was on these paved streets that the town crier sounded the alarm at 10 p.m. every night and warned drunken layabouts to hurry home, even as the windows above were flung open and buckets of waste emptied into the street, the refuse sliding and slithering down to the moat that surrounded the area.

As a result of the terrible rat infestation and the hugely unhygienic conditions of the city, the plague swept through homes, felling rich and poor alike. To save themselves from the spread of the dreaded black death, the wealthy residents who lived above the ground bricked over the entrances to the lower quarters in Mary King's Close, sealing in families living in the underground chambers who had contracted the plague due to their proximity to rats and other vermin. Entire families died of fever and hunger in these underground chambers. Should you book a tour of the underground vaults or a ghost tour on the Royal Mile and step into these spaces, a shiver will run down your spine as you envisage the misery and desperation of those people clawing at the stones and the bricks to escape death.

Ring-a-ring o' roses,
Pocket full of posies,
A-tishoo, a-tishoo,
We all fall down.

This nursery rhyme originated during the plague and gave rise to the macabre game of children holding hands and going round in circles, pretending to sneeze and then dropping to the floor, feigning death. The last one to fall down was made to stand in the centre of the ring in the next round or given a task or punishment.

Depending on the century in which you lived in the city, if you weren't dying of plague or illness, you could well be declared a heretic or Catholic, and either be imprisoned in a steel cage and left out in the square to rot and starve, or get packed into a wooden barrel with iron spikes on both ends and rolled down the cobbled paths to the moat below. If the barrel sank, it was proof that you were a heretic; if it floated and you survived, it meant you were a witch, at which point you were pulled out and burnt at the stake.

Over centuries, this cycle of violence, intrigue and betrayal played out on the blood-soaked streets of Edinburgh, only to give way after World War II to merriment and rejoicing. Mass processions of Hogmanay and the Festival's opening parade featuring jugglers and stilt walkers, clowns and musicians, buskers and acrobats erased from present-day memory the bloody times of the past era. But lurking just below the surface could well be a lonely troll, a disembodied soul, or a headless knight in armour searching for redemption.

Aly, our undercover police officer friend, and Tim, a social worker for the homeless, whom we had met in India on his visit to the Salaam Baalak Trust and become good friends with, snuck us into the Edinburgh Tattoo which was amazing. Thousands sat through a rain-drenched performance of marching bands and military display on the Castle Esplanade, ending with a breathtaking show of fireworks which awed you each evening. Years later, when we were sitting in the Royal Box at the Edinburgh Tattoo with its then director, Brigadier Melville (Mel) Jameson, sipping champagne, our feet covered by a warm tartan blanket as we watched a cast of hundred dancers weave magic to the strains of Indian music, we would reflect back to those adventurous times.

Back then, watching so many different performances, I always wondered why we never saw any work from India. Enthused and inspired by our experience, we returned home exhilarated, exhausted and determined to create a showcase of work that was representative of our classical and contemporary traditions. Teamwork was still in the doldrums, slowly recovering from our decision to move away from our work in TV and return to the arts, and my colleagues swayed between disillusionment and anger at what they thought was my unnecessary use of our limited resources to create an international platform for our shows. It would be some years before we experienced success, and till then the need of the hour was frugality and minimal salaries, which we struggled to pay from month to month.

Thanks to the British Council, I was signed on as guest faculty on a series of art-management workshops led by Roger McCann, and funded in part by Visiting Arts, UK, and the hugely enthusiastic Nelson Fernandez who had fallen in love with India and was keen to promote its culture and arts. With their help, we were able to build a strong network of partners and planned our very first 'Celebrating India Festival' in Edinburgh in 2001. In that first year, we presented six different productions at the Fringe, which met with a modicum of success: music by Indian Ocean at South Side and Out of the Blue; Lillete Dubey's *Dance Like a Man* at Aurora Nova, St. Stephen's; Aditi Mangaldas at the George Square Theatre, etc. The showcase enabled us to network, meet festival directors and venue curators from across the world and host them at the annual dinner we threw for the arts community at our rented apartment—over the years, this became the talk of the town and the must-attend event of the festival. Feeding 150-odd people at an evening do with Indian food and a free bar was unheard of. For us, however, it was a way to showcase

Indian hospitality, with my tribe of assistant chefs, which included Puneeta and our Teamwork colleagues Dilip, Sharupa, Ila, Vandana, Dhruv, Rahul Bali and Rahul Sen, helping out with the cutting and chopping, stirring and washing up, along with Dana Mcleod who was our go-to person for everything in the city and was responsible for borrowing pots and pans from friends to help with the preparation for this feast. Achari potatoes, pork sorpotel, beef chilli, vegetables in a tamarind and turmeric yoghurt sauce and fish in mustard and coconut were staple fare on these occasions.

The dinners were a great success with directors and actors, festival heads and arts managers from Australia and New Zealand, Singapore and London coming over to drink and eat, chat and exchange reviews of the best shows in town. In due course, this led to an even more ambitious plan featuring hundreds of artistes from across all festivals, including the Edinburgh Tattoo, the Edinburgh International Festival, the Edinburgh International Book Festival, the Festival Fringe and the Edinburgh Film Festival.

By 2002, we were showcasing the best of India's performing and visual arts in prime venues across Edinburgh. We had hosted Brian McMaster, the legendary Edinburgh International Festival director, as well as Brigadier Mel Jameson, who came out to India to discover what could be curated for the Edinburgh

Tattoo. Brian loved the idea of doing an all-night Indian classical music presentation at Usher Hall, featuring Pandit Hariprasad Chaurasia on the flute, followed by Hindustani classical vocalist Shruti Sadolikar, and concluding with Ustad Amjad Ali Khan on the sarod in a dusk-to-dawn concert, along with a major exposition of Indian classical dance at the Royal Lyceum Theatre over three nights, bringing together Kathak maestro Birju Maharaj, Bharatanatyam dancer Malavika Sarukkai, the famed Kuchipudi trio Radha, Raja and Kaushalya Reddy, Bharati Shivaji and Vijayalakshmi in a rarely seen lyrical Mohiniyattam performance and Madhavi Mudgal in the Odissi form.

The 2002 edition was a resounding success with sold-out shows, standing ovations and five-star reviews. Ustad Amjad Ali Khan, who was to begin his performance at 3 a.m., was worried no one would stay on and kept sending us slips of paper requesting that he be allowed to go on. When dawn broke, a packed auditorium shrugged off their blankets and were on their feet to stomp and applaud the three great exponents of the Indian classical music tradition who had enthralled a mostly Scottish audience with their virtuoso performances. At the Lyceum Theatre, the aesthetic and graceful turn of Birju Maharaj's wrist was met with rapturous applause and the Mohiniyattam performance, with the dancers dressed in white and gold, had never been seen in Edinburgh before and was much loved. We had come a long way from the time when a dance critic from a Scottish newspaper asked me, 'So Sanjoy, I believe you are going to show us the seven different ways Indians tap their feet in the name of dance!' Annoyed at the ignorance of these critics, we invited them to India to experience the best and worst of our dance forms so that they were educated in its philosophy and artistry.

It had been an adventurous journey from our first hesitant steps at the Fringe opening parade with Aditi Mangaldas perched on a lotus flower on top of an open van, thanks to local grandee Mohinder Dhall, who orchestrated the Indian element in the annual festival parade. Aditi's dancers followed bravely, stopping every now and then to break into their Kathak moves much to Aditi's horror, for she was aghast at the thought of taking this classical dance form from stage to street. She said that her gurus would be horrified by the very thought. My argument was that they would be proud to see how the dance form could be adapted and appreciated by the thousands of people lining Princes Street. Mostly unconvinced, she reluctantly took to promoting Kathak to an audience that had never quite seen anything like it; the act met with great success and over the years she went on to perform in every major international festival across the world.

Our dream to showcase India's diversity grew year on year. We reached out to the Edinburgh International Film Festival and offered to bring in Shah Rukh Khan. The festival agreed and said they would programme him in their theatre on Lothian Road. I demurred and suggested they consider a larger space as the Lothian Road theatre would sell out instantly. They refused, saying that Sean Connery, Pierce Brosnan, Judi Dench, Clint Eastwood, Emma Thompson and other great stars had all been presented there and it would be perfect as a venue. The day the bookings opened, tickets sold out in thirty minutes and made headlines in *The Times*, London, which reported that seats were being sold in the black market at a 100-pound premium. The festival panicked and moved the programme to a 400-seater venue and restricted ticket sales to four per person. These too sold out instantly. Finally, they moved us to a large cinema complex at the edge of the city where Nasreen Munni Kabir, Channel Four's Indian films curator, came up from London to be in conversation with Shah Rukh.

I had notified the police about possible security concerns, but they barely showed any interest and had no idea who Shah Rukh was. For them, it was unthinkable that an Indian film star whom they had never heard of would cause any disruption. Fans who had travelled to Edinburgh lined up at the airport and along the road leading to the venue, screaming and wanting to catch a glimpse of Shah Rukh as he landed at the Edinburgh airport. Thankfully, a senior police officer of Indian descent, realizing the need for security, stepped in and convinced the commissioner that police protection was imperative. But despite the deployment of police and private security, we had to barricade Shah Rukh behind a line of tables at the evening dinner to keep the screaming fans at bay and had to wait it out till the police dispersed the crowds that had gathered outside the host restaurant Suruchi.

At the back of our continued success in Edinburgh and London with shows at Riverside Studios, the South Bank Centre, International Centre for the Arts, Victoria and Albert Museum, etc., Joint Secretary Amitabh Pande of the Department of Science and Technology proposed that we commemorate India's scientific legacy, including showcasing the triangulation instruments which Sir George Everest, after whom the highest peak in the world was named, had first used to measure the mountain peaks of the Himalayan range, at the Cambridge conference held every four years. Amitabh Pande had a panoramic vision, and we set about creating the 'Great Arc Festival', named after John Keay's book on the mapping of the highest mountains of the world, in association with the Department of Science and Technology. High Commissioner Ronen Sen, his erudite and philosophical deputy, Satyabrata

Pal, the newly appointed director of the Nehru Centre, writer–director–actor Girish Karnad, Press Minister Navdeep Suri and his charming wife Mani (who went on to become dear friends and supporters), were all enthusiastic about the festival plan and provided every assistance to make it possible.

Dana Mcleod represented us in Edinburgh and was our go-to person for all advice, local know-how and emergencies. In 2002, the year of the liquid terror attack in Heathrow, our flight landed in the midst of the shutdown. We were transferred to Gatwick without our luggage and were allowed no carry-on bags at check-in. Of the twenty-seven pieces of checked-in luggage that included props and puppets for Dadi Pudumjee's *Transposition*, which we were going to open at Southside, only one piece arrived on the baggage carousel. Dana, our eternal saviour, was at hand to rescue us, providing us some much-needed cash and ferrying us to the many apartments that we had booked to house our ever-expanding tribe of performers. Each day we would head to the airport hoping to spot our luggage from British Airways, but there was to be no such luck; and each day we would have to cancel our show and refund tickets, disappointing audiences. Finally, having given up on the airline, I called Melissa D'Mello, who worked in the Home Office in London, and asked her to use her influence to track our bags. Dana, in the meanwhile, had called the BBC and they did a story on their show *Newshour*. Miraculously, the very next day she received a call from a friend who had just landed at the Edinburgh airport, saying that there were many pieces of strangely shaped bags going round on the baggage carousel with our names on them and that we should retrieve them at the earliest. We rushed over to claim our long-lost puppets and props and finally opened the show that evening.

Of the many houses that Dana sourced for us, the most interesting was the one located at 1 Meadow Place. It was an old church that had been converted into a yoga centre and which doubled as a rehearsal space for us between yoga workshops. There was a house attached to it with its own entrance from 12 Roseneath Place, which was perfect to house the *Transposition* puppeteers and the Nrityagram dancers who were performing at Dance Base, Scotland's National Centre for Dance. Over the years, artistic director Morag Deyes, the reigning queen of Dance Base, had created an amazing institution set in a contemporary building through the glass ceilings of which one could gaze upon the towering Edinburgh Castle above. It was the most prestigious venue to present a dance performance in during the festival.

Bijoyini, Lynne, Sharupa, Puneeta and I occupied the rooms on the top floor of the house and shared a loo, and the others shared bedrooms located at different levels with common baths and toilet facilities in a row downstairs. There was a massive kitchen for cooking and entertaining. As such the house was enormous, though somewhat rundown, and was able to accommodate all of us quite comfortably. The otherwise quiet church-turned-yoga-centre and the attached house were unused to seeing such a flurry of activity. The constant movement of people, late-night partying and morning rehearsals must have disturbed the age-old spirits who inhabited the crevices and spaces between the stone walls and the wooden boards.

In the beginning, there seemed to be a general sense of peace with no real untoward incidents, not a witch nor goblin, Bean Nighe or Glaistig in sight. But as the days passed into weeks, the spirits had probably had enough of us and wanted some peace and quiet, or perhaps they had just decided to be mischievous. One day, in the madness of getting ready, Puneeta left the house keys on the mantle above the fireplace, telling me to pick them up as she stepped out of the door; but when I turned to grab them, they had disappeared. We looked high and low, inside the fireplace and up the chimney, in the dustbin and between the floorboards, in every nook and cranny, but the keys seemed to have vanished into thin air.

The next day, while using the upstairs loo, Lynne hung her churidar on the door hook, only to find that the drawstring had been pulled out. She looked all over, asking us if we had taken it or seen it, but no one had a clue as to what was happening.

These disappearances became a regular event and each of us had to be extra careful while leaving anything in the upstairs rooms. Finally, an exasperated Puneeta demanded that the spirits return the house keys—she ticked them off and told them just how cross she was and that their behaviour was unacceptable and rude! As all of us in the Roy family know, if Puneeta loses her cool, you need to get out of her way. Lo and behold, the keys reappeared on the mantlepiece as did Lynne's churidar's drawstring which was found on the floor of the upstairs loo. The disappearances stopped and peace prevailed. Puneeta relented and sent the spirits love and light, thanked them for the use of their home and apologized for disturbing their peace. I invited them to join us for a show or two and left a glass of brandy every now and then on the mantlepiece. Thereafter, there was harmony in the house and barring frightening Monu, a dancer and puppeteer in the *Transposition* show, by peeping out at him from behind the door when he was working on the computer in a downstairs room, peace prevailed.

Whenever you visit Edinburgh next, make sure you book one of the many underground ghost walks and vault tours on offer. Some are corny, with actors jumping out from behind statues and gravestones in scarlet capes to frighten visitors, but the more historical tours show you a city that lives in many realities and dimensions at the same time with a history which is both violent and dramatic.

As the mist rolls in and the clouds obscure the stars, listen for the haunting strains of the bagpipes being played by a young lad who disappeared hundreds of years ago, or for the rat-a-tat-tat sound that the headless drummer, who was executed for spying, makes as he marches on the ramparts of the Edinburgh Castle.

14

Jahannam—A Visit to Hell

Jerusalem

The Valley of Hinnom is located outside the city walls of Jerusalem. In medieval times it hosted refugees, those who had been evicted or punished, lepers and castaways. The refuse of the city collected here, and it was in every way a living hell filled with vermin, disease and death, plagued by frequent outbreaks of cholera that swept through the congested streets and claimed thousands of lives. This was Jahannam, or Hell, and it was representative of the way the 'people of the Book' envisaged the darkest place where those who had 'sinned' could be banished to and excoriated.

The walled city of Jerusalem is among the most fascinating places in the world. Constantly coveted over its 3,500-year history, it was conquered by King Solomon. It was thereafter ruled over and destroyed in parts by a series of conquerors, from Nebuchadnezzar II to Cyrus the Great, from Alexander, Ptolemy I, Herod, Constantine I and Justinian I to the rulers of the Umayyad dynasty, followed by the Crusaders and Godfrey of Bouillon, until it fell to Sultan Saladdin of the Ayyubid dynasty. The Christians conquered the city from the Abbasids, only for it to be retaken by the Mamluks and the Ottomans.

For millennia, people of the three faiths—Judaism, Islam and Christianity—made their way here as part of their pilgrimage, trudging thousands of miles through forest and desert, crossing mountains and rivers to seek the eternal truth and be blessed; more often than not, they succumbed to the elements on the journey or were killed by bandits who preyed upon the ill-equipped pilgrims or they died in the many battles that dominated the bloody history of the city.

The evening glow of the setting sun, reflecting off the iridescent white sandstone walls shimmering like the burnished shields of a thousand men riding into battle, with flags hoisted high atop the battlements, it seemed more a sign of conquest than welcome. Jaffa Gate is straddled by modern monuments to Mammon: high-walled malls with sanitized restaurants, crowded with thirsty tourists intent on capturing on their phones their breathless march in Jesus's footsteps, oblivious to the history of bloodshed, plunder, power and despair all around them. As you enter the gate and navigate through the narrow streets with overhanging balconies adorned by the washing of the day, the smell of perfumed hookahs, spiced kebabs and Eastern sweetmeats mingled with aromatic Arabic coffee fills your senses.

You can stroll through the Armenian quarters, past the kosher Jewish restaurants, the cross streets with the Coptic, the Russian Orthodox, the Ethiopian and the Muslim quarters, the higgledy-piggledy cafés and shops piled one on top of the other with partially hidden stairways leading to nowhere and cracks in the wall revealing underground caves and passages cut into the hill over millennia, offering up the possibility of secret chambers filled with ancient scrolls; and you would wonder how anyone, man or god, could possibly untangle the politics and history of the march of mankind across 3,500 years. Which president could offer a solution to this collective complexity and passion? Who would know how to undo a stitch in the fabric of time and straighten out a million threads that make this one of the greatest cities in the world that so many emperors and rulers have wished to conquer, possess, destroy, rebuild or experience?

In 2011, I received a call from Ambassador Navtej Sarna who, having been India's external affairs spokesperson, was keen to leverage India's smart power and had envisioned a festival full of wonder, tapping into Israel's love for India and hippiedom. Pre-Covid, approximately 60,000 Israelis visited India annually after their indoctrination into the army as part of their compulsory service programme. Two years of extensive mind-numbing training was meant to erase empathy from their souls, as we have seen in the horrors committed by Israeli soldiers in the ongoing genocide in Gaza. After the training, they used to flee from their kibbutz and the intense pressure and discipline and revel in the comparative gentleness of an ancient philosophy, experience the heavenly beaches of Goa, the cool climes of Kullu and Manali and other electrifying experiences that India has to offer.

Looking forward to discovering Jerusalem, I flew out to Tel Aviv to explore its vibrant performing and visual arts scene, the dynamic dance companies at the Suzanne Dellal Centre for Dance and Theatre, the design and art galleries that surround it, the Cameri Theatre, the Jaffa clock tower with what has to be the best offering of a stuffed shoulder of lamb, the Cinematheque, the

Tel Aviv port area repurposed as a design district and the many public and private museums that the city boasts of.

The drive to Jerusalem from Tel Aviv was disconcerting. Faceless concrete walls topped by enraged Medusa heads of coiled barbed wire, reminiscent of the concentration camps that Jews were corralled into, divided the Palestinian territories from Israel. Our driver pointed out that homes topped with white synthetic water tanks were Jewish, while those with black ones were Palestinian. Heavily guarded checkpoints ensured the incarceration of a people who had few civil or human rights and were subjected to daily humiliations, with minimal access to jobs and medical intervention, often shot or arrested and 'worked over' for resisting oppression or for voicing dissent.

New Jerusalem was no different from any small European city, with multi-storeyed hotels and business centres, broad streets and ordered traffic leading off to quieter neighbourhoods with two-storeyed homes shuttered from public view by high walls and gates, hiding their own secrets.

As you drive up to Mishkenot Sha'ananim, the India International Centre (IIC) of Jerusalem, you pass an incongruous Dutch-styled windmill built in 1857 by Sir Moses Montefiore as a flour mill to help the Jews of Palestine become self-supporting. Sadly, the venture wasn't a success as there were few windy days in the area and the windmill fell to ruin before it was restored under British mandate in the 1930s. During the 1948 civil war, the Jewish resistance built a watchtower on top of it, which the British demolished, stating that it was a security threat. The attempt to do so was dubbed 'Operation Don Quixote' by the local population. When the soldiers who happened to be from a regiment from Ramsgate, England, reached the battlements and read the plaque naming Montefiore, who hailed from their town, as the sponsor, they reinterpreted their orders and only blew up the observation tower. In 2012, the mill was completely restored and is now a museum, marking the entrance to the centre.

A winding paved road takes you down to the gate of the Mishkenot which was the first construction to be built outside the walls of the city, made possible by a donation by Judah Touro to Sir Moses Montefiore. The building, made of Jerusalem stone mined by Arab Christians from Bethlehem, was designed by architect W.R. Smith. The red tiles were imported from Marseille and the ornate iron arches and grilles were ordered from Montefiore's own hometown of Ramsgate.

The sixteen apartments, with two rooms each and a kitchen, were completed by 1861, as were the two synagogues, one for the Ashkenazic Jews and the other for the Sephardic Jews, along with a well which had a small hand pump that people came to see and marvel at, all built at a princely cost of 6,000 pound sterling. In the centre of the building, on top of the stone façade was inscribed: '*Mishkenot Sha'ananim was established with the money bequeathed by the benefactor Judah Touro, may his soul rejoice in Eden.*'

While the settlement was ready to receive its first occupants, it took a while to tempt families to move there as they were extremely reluctant to leave the old city. The few who did, came during the day and left at night before the city gates shut. The road to the old city was dangerous and a resident was murdered trying to chase away marauders who viewed the settlement and its Jewish inhabitants as fair game. The defeat of the Ottoman Empire embittered the local population against the Jews and thousands were banished or forced to flee and others paid a ransom to avoid being drafted into the Turkish army. Typhoid took its toll even as food supplies dried up and an infestation of locusts overran the country. During the battle for Jerusalem in 1917, the residents of Mishkenot took refuge in the old city and, in doing so, were saved, as the British had decided against the bombing of the holy sites.

In 1966, the then mayor of Jerusalem and the Jerusalem Foundation ordered the buildings to be restored as a centre for the arts, and in 1973 the place was opened to artistes and creative people from across the world to stay and innovate, to share their expertise and exchange views with their Israeli counterparts. It was here that we were to jointly host our new initiative, 'Words on Water', during the Festival of India in Israel.

When I arrived at Mishkenot it was early evening and the light from the setting sun had cast a soft golden hue on Jerusalem's stone walls, topped by the golden Dome of the Rock. Deep in the valley, a rock concert was starting up. Jahannam had long been converted into a park and entertainment arena that hosted concerts and cultural performances.

The suite of rooms that I checked into were sparse yet beautifully appointed with lamps casting a warm light on the sandstone walls and the beds covered in crisp white sheets. Sleeping in an unfamiliar space is always an effort for me. I have a routine which includes switching off as many lights inside and outside the room as I can before going to sleep. Having done so, I settled down with Simon Sebag Montefiore's *Jerusalem: The Biography*, a must-read book for anyone with an interest in history and wishing to understand the complexities of the clash of civilizations and religions. Having read a bit, I turned off my bedside lamp, donned my eye mask and placed a pillow on my head, hoping to convey to my brain that it was time to sleep. Restless and overloaded by the sights and the smells, I needed to calm down and did a set of breathing exercises to control my heartbeat, followed by a short meditation that would help me doze off.

There was a stillness in the air. Even the stone walls, cooled to a comfortable 18 degrees Celsius by the air-conditioning, seemed to be holding their breath. In my half-dream state, I was wondering if I was awake or asleep when I felt the collective pain and anguish of countless souls oozing from the cracks of the stone wall where they had been trapped, reaching out to surround me, encircling my ankles and wrists, their tentacles wrapping themselves around my neck, making me gag.

My eyes opened to darkness. I struggled to move, remove my eye mask and throw away the pillow as the terror of the moment alerted every cell in my body. I pushed back, my muscles tensed, but I was now pinned down and something seemed to be forcing itself upon me. The pressure on my entire being was such that I had to struggle to breathe; my limbs were immobile, my mind numb with panic, a scream frozen in the back of my throat. Sweating from every pore, I made an attempt to sit up and get off the bed—anything to get away from the presence bearing down on me, but I just couldn't do so. Exhausted, I finally gave in and felt the presence enter me and take over my body till it had become one with me. I was terrified that this was the Rishikesh experience repeating itself and I was being possessed yet again, or was I having a heart attack, given the immense pressure on my chest?

Somehow, I finally jumped out of bed, scrabbled for the light switch, and lurched to the living room, my heart beating rapidly. I opened my bag and took out the sacred memorabilia that I had received from the priest at the Church of the Holy Sepulchre earlier in the day, and sprinkled holy water around my bed, wore the cross and the beads blessed by the clergyman and placed the image of Jesus and Mother Mary under my pillow—all the while chanting, '*Namah Shivaiay namaha, namoh Vishnu, namoh Narayan, namoh namaha.*'

The next morning, I called Puneeta and related what had happened and asked that she speak with Gurudev to make sense of the night's experience and to let me know what steps I needed to take to rid myself of the energy that had possessed me. Some hours later, Puneeta called back with instructions to cover myself in a column of purple and gold light which would protect me when I travelled as I was susceptible to dark energies. Gurudev had said that I had been possessed by a good spirit, a wise soul, Moses-like, who was there to protect me from the dark energies I had attracted and that I shouldn't worry. I had been sent to Jerusalem to clear some past karma and heal the space, Gurudev had said. He had also said that Puneeta would take me through a guided meditation and asked that I receive healing energies and, in turn, send back love and light from my heart chakra to the many souls who remained trapped in the area. I remained incredulous and in a state of disbelief at the thought of Moses having possessed me.

Feeling refreshed after a hot bath, I sat down to meditate, still wondering why Moses, of all people, had come to me. Ready for the day after the guided meditation session, I walked out of the room. The sun had risen, bathing the city walls in gold that reflected off its domes and minarets. A new day had broken with the possibility of more adventure and discovery as I headed out past Herod's Gate and went to visit the Indian hospice located within the city walls, where Baba Farid had once lived and meditated.

As I walked through the antiquated streets in the old city, I did so knowing that I needed to tread softly, as I was treading on the dreams and hopes of so many who had fought in the bloody wars and skirmishes over millennia, a war that shows no sign of letting up even now as we helplessly witness the horror of the ongoing genocide and the murder of so many innocent people.

Recently, when I was researching the background of Mishkenot Sha'ananim for this chapter, I discovered the uncanny fact that the original name for the settlement was Kerem Moshe—the Vineyard of Moses!

15

The Apparition

Valladolid

The gentle flutter of white fabric may have woken me up; even as my fogged and jet-lagged brain clawed its way out of the abyss and tried to focus, I knew there hadn't been any curtains in the archway that separated the bedroom from the living area. As my vision adjusted to the darkness, I perceived a pair of kohl-dipped eyes assessing me inquisitively. I sat up in bed, embarrassed by this unannounced guest. I smiled and looked back, wanting to ask if they were from housekeeping, and realized that the smudged-out face had neither nose nor neck, nor any determinate form. As I continued to take in the presence of this intruder, I discovered that it didn't have hands or legs either. In any other situation, I would have screamed and leapt from the bed, frightened out of my wits, and reached for the lights. But there was something quite calm and unintrusive about the apparition in the doorway that, in turn, helped calm my panic.

It was a cold night in 2004 at the Hospedería del Colegio de Santa Cruz in the city of Valladolid, a historic annexe to the Colegio Mayor Santa Cruz, one of Spain's oldest university colleges, founded in 1484 by Cardinal Pedro González de Mendoza. The Hospedería, constructed in 1675, was intended to accommodate former students who had completed their eight-year residency at the college but needed to remain in Valladolid while awaiting academic, ecclesiastical or legal appointments.

Earlier that day, I had flown into Madrid and taken the fast train from Chamartín, travelling through the snow-clad mountains of the Sierra de Guadarrama, and passing through the historic town of Segovia before arriving in Valladolid, the erstwhile capital of Spain. Valladolid was rich in history dating back to the eleventh century, when the Church of Santa Maria de la Antigua and the Puente Mayor bridge were built by Count Pedro Ansurez. Archaeological findings date the area back to 200 BCE and connect it to pre-Roman tribes, known as the Valle del Lid, who inhabited the area. It was ruled by the Moors until 1208, when it became a cultural centre and the court of King Alfonso VIII. Christopher Columbus died here; the legendary Spanish writer Cervantes, who wrote the classic *Don Quixote*, lived here and was arrested briefly; and Ferdinand and Isabel were engaged here in the Palace of Los Vivero and merged the kingdoms of Castille and Lyon to set the foundations of the Spanish Empire.

In 1478, Ferdinand and Isabella established the Spanish Inquisition, a tribunal targeting Conversos Jews who had converted to Christianity but were suspected of practising their original faith in secret, as well as Protestant Moriscos or Muslims who had converted to Christianity. A confession was obtained by torture and the use of iron masks, hand and feet screws, nail removers and caskets with nails in which you were impaled and flayed till you confessed or were killed. Those found guilty of heresy were punished and burnt at the stake.

By the mid-sixteenth century, the Inquisition had cracked down on Protestant communities in Valladolid and Seville and had persecuted a group of mystics—the Alumbrados—for their alleged heretical beliefs and literature, as the spread of heretical ideas through books was prohibited and banned.

I had been invited by the ever-energetic Guillermo Rodriguez (Emo), who had travelled to India to study in Kerala with his exquisitely talented partner Monica de la Fuente, a Flamenco dancer who went on to study Bharatanatyam. They had returned to Valladolid in the late 1990s to set up Casa de la India, a cultural and educational institution which envisioned closer ties with India through the exploration of its arts, culture and knowledge traditions in partnership with the city and the University of Valladolid.

Casa de la India was a short walking distance from the Valladolid train station. Its red brick exteriors and warm wood flooring, with a crimson-streaked silk wall covering, floor cushions, rich carpets and a bronze Ganesha sculpture brought you home to India. The brick-paved courtyard had a façade of a traditional Gujarati wooden haveli, complete with a balcony which had been shipped from India as a gift by the city of Ahmedabad.

As long-term partners of this institution, Emo had wanted us to collaborate on projects and meet with the mayor and Valladolid's university partners. Together, we hosted the annual Spanish film festival in India, created the first digital art presentation on the occasion of Arco—Spain's commercial arts fair—and extended our footprint to Barcelona, which hosted our popular musical, *Bollywood Love Story*, at the Teatro Victoria, where it was sold out for weeks on end.

Walking back from Casa de la India to the university, you strolled through the Campo Grande, Valladolid's central park, with peacocks and peahens, holm oaks and cork oaks, pines, poplars, willows and alders, their leaf-shorn branches reaching for porcelain blue skies. Citizens gathered here with babies in prams and elders in shrouds of grey and black, hunched against the cold winds blowing across snow-clad mountains; young kids played on the sidewalk while couples looked into each other's eyes as they romanced on park benches or at the medieval water fountain. You crossed the street into the old town, characterized by its Castilian architecture, and headed towards the San Pablo Church with its impressive façade and stunning stained-glass windows, past the university square with its many lions on pedestals which you were never to count as it brought you bad luck in your exams, and to the entrance of the university. As you stepped through the enormous doors into the Santa Cruz Palace, you could see the chapel on the right with the iconic figure of The Christ of Light, sculpted by Gregorio Fernandez, set against a red tapestry, blood trickling down from its ribs, shoulders and knees in a life-like imitation of the crucifixion.

I have always found visiting a new town and exploring its architectural and historical landmarks, savouring new dishes and immersing myself in its culture fascinating. The mayor of Valladolid had hosted an official dinner which began at 9 p.m. at a 150-year-old restaurant famous for its meats. The first round of gammon, cured and sliced ham, arrived with an array of starters and tapas, and this was followed by soup served up in a tureen the equivalent of a bathtub; a whole fillet of fish in olive oil, garlic and rosemary came next, and thereafter arrived half a roasted pig and a whole ewe roasted in its juices with the meat falling off the bone. Each dish was accompanied with a bottle of the vintage Castellon red wine that the region was known for. When the last course of steak arrived, it was well past midnight and I was ready to go straight to food heaven. I knew if I ate even one more morsel, I would definitely throw up and spend a restless night trying to digest the enormous feast.

It was much after 2 a.m. when I staggered back to the university quarters. I could almost smell on the paved streets the blood of the countless heretics who had been scoured and marched through to the city square to their ultimate death. I carefully navigated the steps up to the first floor and let myself into the corner room, its stone floor and walls echoing a history going back 600 years. I had a combination of Carbo Veg and Ipecac—homoeopathy remedies for acidity and overeating—and crawled into bed, jetlagged and drunk. The sheets were crisp and white, the pillow overstuffed, and I sank into them and drifted away to never-never land.

The awareness that someone was in the room grew upon me even as I slept, and I struggled to open my eyes and focus my wine-soaked brain on my immediate surroundings. The slight swish of white fabric where there shouldn't have been any caught my attention, and I sat upright in bed. The presence stared back and didn't seem to be hostile in any sense, more inquisitive in fact, with a certain gentle air that relaxed me. I finally managed to ask if I could be of any help, but this elicited no response, just more gazing.

I took in the image, not sure if this was a man or a woman. The spirit seemed young and composed, unlike any I had encountered before. There was no sense of hysteria, anger, trauma or urgency to communicate, just a sense of peaceful coexistence. I tried to tune into its thoughts and found that I couldn't. I wondered if I was in fact awake, and gently ran my fingers through my hair, thinking of what I should do next. I looked towards the bedside lamp and contemplated switching it on, but when I looked back the image had disappeared, only to reappear at the window draped with heavy curtains.

I wasn't sure if it had been a few minutes or more when I switched on the lamp and the apparition disappeared. I drank a glass of water—my mouth was parched and my body felt dehydrated from the wine—got back into bed and dreamt of a group of mystics, singing beautifully, gathered on the banks of a stream and making their way across a stone bridge with lanterns in their hand.

Many years later, in 2022, when we launched JLF Spain, one of the many receptions was hosted on the banks of the Pisuerga river that flows through the city: a river I had never known existed, with a stone bridge built over it which was one of the early constructions in the region. As I was researching the history of the city and the university with the help of Paloma Castro, the vice rector in charge of international relations, who made available the necessary research documents, I came upon some details of the Inquisition which described the persecution of a group of mystics, the Alumbrados, who used to practise in this area.

And I remembered the stone bridge and the lantern-carrying mystics I had seen in my dream that night.

16

Pirates

Maldives

In 2020, we had been introduced by Shobhaa Dé to Sonu and Eva Shivdasani, the visionary owners of the Soneva Island Resorts in the Maldives and in Thailand. Previously, they had run the Sixth Senses spa chain before selling it off, only to reinvest in a few islands in the northwest of the Maldivian archipelago. Their sense of design, the service at the property and the varied cuisine on offer were unmatched and they remain the gold standard of hospitality among resorts in the world.

Having agreed to come out for two days to explore the possibility of hosting a JLF in the Maldives, we arrived in Malé in 2021, amidst the ongoing Covid pandemic. As we stepped off the plane into what still appeared to be a provincial airport, we were received by the Soneva team who whisked us away to the seaport lounge and pampered us with fragrant towels, delicious cookies and chocolates, fresh juices and sandwiches. We then boarded the Soneva seaplane and were transported across the ocean, which was dotted with small islands, emerald-blue lagoons and sandy white beaches fringed with palm trees.

At the Soneva International Airport, we stepped off onto a floating wooden raft bobbing gently in the middle of the vast waters. From there we were taken on a speed boat to the resort island, which was a ten-minute ride, dependent somewhat on the weather of the day. As the host team collected our shoes and socks and helped us with the life jackets, we knew that this was going to be a special experience.

Soneva Fushi has an understated elegance with a quality of luxury that's difficult for any resort to attain. Over the years, the island had been greened into a wonderful forest with large banyan groves, lantana and palm trees, and had villas sporting plunge pools, open-air showers, private beaches, speciality chocolate and ice-cream rooms, cheese, meat and salad bars, apart from a number of restaurants offering a variety of to-die-for cuisines.

Given the Covid situation, we were escorted to our individual villas by our butlers, tested for the virus and asked to stay there till our test results came in the next day. Each villa was fully appointed with a living area, study, bedroom, porch and balcony where you could settle down with a glass of wine and watch the sun rise or set and observe the most amazing marine life flit in and out of the corals and sandbanks. Hammerhead sharks, parrot fish and sting rays by the dozen, and on a lucky day a giant tortoise might decide to take a paddle in your swimming pool as a break from its daily routine. The sandy paths that were cleaned through the day allowed us to sense the earth beneath our feet, creating a charm and a sense of well-being that few other properties in the world can boast of.

As our villas were on the same stretch of the beach, Sharupa, Ankur and I met for dinner in my palatial suite of rooms and thereafter headed out for an exploratory walk along the pristine white shore, feeling carefree and blessed to have this amazing opportunity in the midst of the pandemic. The soft crunch of the sand, the waves lapping gently over our feet even as thousands of plankton glowed in the dark, made for a magical and ethereal experience.

Right before stepping out of the room, I had placed my handmade black leather Janota juttis just inside the bedroom door. We returned around midnight after a long meandering walk on the beach, only to find these missing. Assuming I must have left them someplace else, I didn't give it much thought till the next morning when I searched for them in every room of my villa, but to no avail. Since the island is out of bounds for anybody but guests and the resort staff, this was puzzling. The next day, Shifaz, my wonderful personal butler, looked high and low and put the word out throughout the resort to try and trace the missing juttis, but with no success. Given that Janota, who made bespoke handmade slip-ons, had shut down for the time, these were truly precious to me: I loved the soft camel leather that was treated with care, the hand-polished and cured soles and the curve with a slash of red in the front, and was very sad to have lost them.

That evening, after a customary swim in the ocean outside my room and a dip in my warm swimming pool, I put my swimming trunks out to dry on the wooden rack in the vast open-air bathroom that came with a paddling pool, an outdoor and indoor shower and a luxurious bathtub. The next morning, I woke up to find my swimming trunks on the far end of the wading pool with the drawstring removed. I assumed it must have been an inquisitive crow or seagull that was responsible and thought nothing of it. But even after leaving the island, I kept following up with Shifaz regarding the whereabouts of my juttis, which seemed to have vapourized forever.

We had two wonderful editions of JLF at Soneva, each spread over two weeks; the festival featured some of the world's best writers and musicians and served up the most amazing food. Film screenings under the stars at the open-air Cinema Paradiso, with surround sound and a feast featuring recipes inspired by the films we screened, including *Monsoon Wedding*, *Slumdog Millionaire* and *Call Me by Your Name*, were truly memorable. The seafood at Out of the Blue and the organic dishes at Fresh from the Garden, prepared by Michelin-starred chefs, were unmatched, especially when clubbed with visits to the observatory following a talk by astrophysicist Priyamvada Natarajan. In Aroon Purie's words, 'It was truly a feast for the mind, body and soul!'

Given that we knew the island well and had stayed in different villas over our many visits, it was somewhat disconcerting when, after having checked in for the festival, I felt uncomfortable and restless through the night in the villa allocated to us. Puneeta ascribed it to the bed and felt that maybe it was too soft or that the mattress didn't suit us. This was instantly addressed by the butler who had the mattress changed and a hardboard placed underneath, and yet the sense of heaviness and discomfort persisted. Tossing and turning as I do on most nights, I dreamt of pirates boarding ships in distress, swords clashing, the smell of gunpowder, and fights to the death as the marauders overpowered the traders and sailors. I awoke mid-dream, walked out to the balcony and peered into the darkness, hoping to calm my beating heart with the sound of the ocean which I so love, but it didn't work. A heaviness seemed to have permeated our beautiful villa, and it was made worse one night when while heading to the outdoor loo, I fell into the deep stone bathtub, injured my leg, and limped through the rest of the week.

The next morning, while we were listening to Pranay Lal—an Indian biochemist and environmentalist whose book *Indica* is about the deep natural history of the subcontinent, with references to the formation of the Maldivian archipelago and its 1,200-plus coral or sandbank islands—I shared my unease with Eva, Sonu's wonderful partner and co-owner of the resort. Eva mentioned that the side of the island that we were staying on this time was once used by pirates as a graveyard and that she and Sonu too had occasionally sensed a kind of negative energy and experienced strange happenings in a villa they had lived in while the resort was being built.

My ability to sniff out negative energy and engage with souls who need healing has often placed me in an uncomfortable position. Walking into the newly built home of a friend, I had found the energy under their stunning floating marble staircase—which was straight out of *Architectural Digest*—to be a problem, as was the energy of the kitchen garden and the vast expanse of lawn at the back of the house. Some years later, after tragedy visited the family, I offered unsolicited advice on what needed to be done to address the issue: keep a diya lit at all times, and move the kitchen garden, as it had been planted on burial ground.

In the early years of the KRC, I received messages from the universe for the participants of the weekly Sunday meditation sessions which we regularly attended; I chose not to share these messages with the people they were aimed at as I was unsure about how the messages would be received. When I discussed my dilemma with Puneeta and Urmila, they said that it was my responsibility to pass these messages and to do so in an unedited form. I still couldn't bring myself to do so. How do you tell a person that she was going to have a heart attack, or, in another instance, that the person had cancer and needed an urgent medical intervention? I often ended up circumnavigating the actual issue and coming up with a rather lame, 'Have you been well?' or 'When did you have your last check-up?' and 'Perhaps you should visit your doctor?' As it happened, both recipients were much wiser than me and more accepting of the messages from the universe—they did go for their check-ups, leading to medical intervention well in time.

On the second evening of our recce at Soneva, we caught up for drinks with a couple and their daughter who were on holiday and had been on the same flight as us. A glass of wine later, I had messages pouring through for the lady which I relayed, much to the surprise of the couple. It took some time for them to ingest what I said about their relationship with their absentee son and their overwhelming sense of guilt and inadequacy as parents. It resulted in a fairly tumultuous night for them as they dealt with underlying issues that they hadn't addressed. While messages continue to come through to me, I still feel diffident about sharing them with those intended to be the recipients.

Puneeta and I have always been fortunate to have the company and support of our friends and family and the protection of our spirit guides who have been integral to our lives. Our first-born cat Prithvi (affectionately called Puddy) arrived during Covid, left behind by his mother on the ledge in our backyard. Over time, we coaxed him to come down and drink milk and have some cat food.

One day, a gaggle of monkeys arrived and tried to steal him, pulling at the wailing kitten through the bars. Puneeta did her best to drive them away and moved Puddy, who was a trembling ball of fur, into one of the downstairs bedrooms. Being a feral cat, he never allowed us to touch him and would strike out with his claws; the only way to interact with him was to play the stick game: push one of Avik's discarded drumsticks under his bed or cat cave, at which point he would try and pounce on it and play with us.

One day, Puddy disappeared and didn't return for days. Puneeta was heartbroken and drove around the colony looking for him in the many parks in the area. At night, we would leave food in his bowl and keep the bedroom door leading to the back garden open, should he return.

Ten days later, in the middle of the night, I heard the maddest of yowls and opened the door to see a cat fight taking place on the neighbour's parapet, fur flying, claws slashing, screeching and hissing as only two tabbies can do. I knew it was Puddy, and Puneeta and I called out to him while chasing the other cat away. He came scampering in and leapt upon the food we had set out for him. He was bedraggled, bloodied and dirty, obviously hadn't eaten for days and sported many a battle scar.

It was a changed Puddy who had returned to us, gentle and loving, wanting to be petted and scratched, cuddled (up to a point) and loved, never wanting to leave Puneeta's side. He appeared wise and empathetic, especially in comparison to our girls Tara and Megh, who Puneeta had brought back from her sister's house where their cat had delivered a new litter, to keep Puddy company. The girls are beautiful, and Tara plays the entitled princess while Megh is a gentle loving soul. Sadly, they both hate Puddy who used to jump on them when they were kittens.

Intrigued about our connection with Puddy, Puneeta asked Gurudev about his significance in our lives. Gurudev told her that he was our soul guide sent to look out for us, to make sure we feel we are never alone, and to remind us of the power of the energy of love. Strange are the ways of the universe.

Acknowledgements

The idea of my writing a book first came up years ago at a lunch with Renuka Chatterjee at the Oriental Octopus, when she urged me to pen down my adventures with food. Since then, various offers had come my way, which made me turn to Hemali Sodhi at A Suitable Agency, whom I have always admired. In discussions with Hemali and Ranjana Sengupta, we settled on the idea of writing about my encounters with the supernatural. Throughout the process of writing, they stood by me, editing the manuscript and making it submission-ready, and held my hand through my trials and tribulations of writing anything at all. Deep gratitude to both for the trust, patience and support.

Thanks to the dynamic and ever-energetic Ananth Padmanabhan who has grown the very idea of publishing in India; to Udayan Mitra who painstakingly edited the manuscript with Prerna, Shatarupa and Gayatri who helped shape it in the way it is—and for some reason believes that the book works; to Bonita who designed the many versions of the cover; and to Akriti, Aman and the entire HarperCollins team for taking this book to the world.

Life is stranger than fiction, and I have had the privilege of experiencing this across many continents, in several countries and cities, and have encountered on the way some extraordinary people who have enriched our lives with their stories, love and hospitality. Among them are Anne Buddle in Edinburgh whose home has always been open for us, and Dana Mcleod, our soul sister, who loves India; Nelson Fernandez from Visiting Arts who helped bring to reality the idea of a 'Festival of India' in Edinburgh; Veronica Hall who spread the word; Jay Shah of the Mahindra Group who is amongst the biggest advocates of the cultural sector; and Sushma Bahl, the pioneering arts professional in India who nudged me to look beyond our shores. My thanks also to the bands Indian Ocean, Mrigya, Parikrama and Advaita; to the musicians Shubha Mudgal and Aneesh

Pradhan, Dr L. Subramaniam and Kavita Krishnamurti, Pandit Hariprasad Chaurasia, Shubhendra Rao and Saskia Rao-de Haas, Vidya Shah, Sonam Kalra, Chugge Khan, Nathoo Lal Solanki, Kutle Khan; to the dancers from Nrityagram and Protima Gauri Bedi, Aditi Mangaldas, the late Astad Deboo, Daksha Seth, Gilles Chuyen; and to Dadi Pudumjee and the Ishara Puppet Theatre Trust who walked a difficult path and created magic.

Thanks to my co-directors at the Jaipur Literature Festival, Namita Gokhale and William Dalrymple.

To the masters of creativity, Shah Rukh and Gauri Khan, Sharmila Tagore, Shekhar Kapur, Shabana Azmi, Manoj Bajpayee, Nandita Das, Shashi Tharoor and the numerous other talented artistes, writers, musicians and painters who have filled our lives with joy, amusement and amazement.

To longtime supporters, funders and believers in the arts: Faith and John Singh of the Jaipur Virasat Foundation, and Surina and H.S. Narula who were Jaipur Literature Festival's first major sponsors.

To Teamwork's first investor board: Rajeev Agrawal, Siddharth Kedia, Atul Kunwar, Nirmesh Prakash, Amit Maloo and Mangesh from Ambit Pragma who in 2013 envisioned that the creative sector was worth investing in. To the dynamic Ashok and Reena Wadhwa who continue to support the vision. To Naushad

Forbes, Denzil Desouza and Chello, Maulik and Richa Sharedalal, Kamini and Vindi Banga who stepped in with their unstinting support; Sanjay and Jyoti Agarwal with their Midas touch and their love for everything Jaipur who helped us understand the business of the arts; TWA's serving board members Shailly Gupta, Sushant Bhansali and advisor Govind Saboo.

To friends who have over the years hosted us, believed in celebrating India through its arts and collaborated in establishing pioneering festivals from Indonesia and Israel through South Africa and Switzerland, Australia and Canada: Navdeep and Mani Suri, Avina and Navtej Sarna, Sanjay and Ranu Bhattacharyya, Masakui Rungsung and Sweety, Vikas and Aparna Swarup, Pavan and Renu Verma, Vikram and Sangeeta Doraiswami, Sanjay and Sangeeta Matta, Pinak and Radha Chakravarty, Shyam and Anita Saran, Harsh Vardhan Shringla, Dinesh and Poonam Patnaik.

To our theatre fraternity from TAG: artistic director and mentor Barry John, fellow travellers Annie Thomas, Asha Kochar, Amit Bhatia, Benny Thomas, Bharat Kapoor, Babu and Rosa Basu, Bapu Sircar, Cecil Qadir, Deepak Mukarji, Deepika Deshpande, Divya Seth, Laila Tyabji, Lillete and Ravi Dubey, Lynne Fernandez, Mekhala Deva, Mona Rao, Pamela Rooks, Premila Nazareth, Rahul Mookerjee, Ranganathan, Revathy and Venkatraman, Riaz bhai, Sita Raina, Varun Sood,

Vidyun Singh, Viveka Kumari, Sujata Subramanium, Gayathri Viswanathan and a brood of thespians with whom we explored theatre, performance and life.

To school friends Anita Priyadarshini, Ayesha Mishra, Bulbul Singh, Manisha Chaudhry, Sujata 'Rags' Raghavan, Vikram and Srinka Wallia and college mates Manoj Saxena, Samir Sahu and Madhav Dar.

To my teachers and professors who shaped me and who should be blamed for all that I have done: Mrs Jeffries, Vijaya Ghose, Prem Krishnan, Dr Gupta, Dr Vohra and Dr Vijay Tankha.

To my first and only bosses at B.V. Videographics, film producers Varsha and Bobby Bedi.

To Teamwork co-founder Mohit Satyanand who never faltered in his belief that TWA would be a sustainable model, and to our founding group: Charu Sharma, Deepika Deshpande, Rituraj Singh and Sant Ram.

To my colleagues who have journeyed with me through challenging times: Sharupa 'CD' Dutta who has travelled the distance, bullied me and yet kept the faith; Ankur Bhardwaj who promised to work hard till one day I would only travel first class; Ila Gupta, Rahul Sen and Debaraj who worked through so many cycles at Teamwork, including near-bankruptcy, and yet never tired nor jumped ship. To Arundhati Nath, Deepika Gandhi, Dinesh, Jamie Mehra, Judith, Kritika Gupta,

Maushmi, Manoj, Minhal Hassan, Niharika, Preeta Singh, Rajatri, Rajinder, Raveena, Rajan, Ruchika, Sandeep, Sammohan Mathodia, Shams Jawaid, Sheuli Sethi, Shiju, Shivaji, Sunil Gupta, Suraj Dhingra, Sanjay Sachdeva, Tarun Laroia, Tavishi, Ujan, Uttam, Vandana Verma, Vasundhara Mehta, Viraj, Yamini and countless other colleagues both past and present who continue to keep the wheels of our many festivals running.

To Shweta Asnani, who took Teamwork to Singapore and Rohit Narang, friend and funder; Lakshmi Laroia who wrote our first film scripts and commissioned one of India's first game shows *Tol Mol Ke Bol*; and Nishta Sipahimalani who extended our reach to Hong Kong through the films and festivals we have produced together; and Gokul Laroia who opened his heart and home to us.

To the originators of Friends of Music which lives on in people's hearts and souls even to this day and which set us off on our journey in creating platforms for the arts: Kanika Satyanand, Val Shipley and Mohit.

To my colleagues at Salaam Baalak Trust (SBT) who have worked selflessly to provide safe spaces for street and working children to realize their full potential; to fellow co-founders Praveen Nair and Mira Nair, and trustees Anubhav Nath, Ashok Pal Singh, Gagan Singh and Geetan Batra; to our institution heads Anjani

Tiwari and Shikha Maini; our key colleagues Dr Amit Sen, Dr Mishra, Anjou Chopra and Tanya Alagh; and our amazing SBT staff and alumni who have taught us empathy, positivity and resilience: Anand, Anju, Babloo, Danish, Durgesh, Haran, Gagan, Noor, Neetu, Pankaj, Pawan, Pramod, Praveen, Khursheed, Kumari, Khusboo, Lakshmi, Rajendar, Ravi, Rizwan, Rohit, Rekha, Resham, Ritesh, Salim, Salman, Santosh, Shanaz, Shravan, Shameem, Shahdutt, Shamsul, Shekhar, Shiv Kumar, Shivalik, Shravan, Sonia, Sunil, Sudhir, Sanjay, Uttam, Vicky, Vivek, Vijay and Viraj.

To my late parents Aparajita and Admiral M.K. 'Micky' Roy for showing us the world and allowing us to discover it on our own terms, while instilling in us a deep-seated philosophy of equity and justice, tradition and selfless service.

To my mamu and mami Abhimanyu and Indrani Gooptu; Arpita and Sanjoy Sen; my aunts, uncles, cousins, nieces and nephews; the Gooptus, Sens and Mallicks who have been more than family and who continue to keep us rooted to the idea of the 'Bangali bhadrolok', however faded that image may be today.

To my late in-laws, the gentle Satya and Vimla Bhushan, who were initially apprehensive of how this 'theatrewalla' with no other day job would take care of their daughter, and who are hopefully more at peace now. To my sister-in-law and brother-in-law Poonam and Sunil Mehra, along with their beautiful, eccentric brood: Nidhi, Akhil, Jamie, Divyansh, Samara, Ishana and Atreya.

To the Roy and Gupta cousins: Nipu (Tuhin) and Tinni (Bhaswati), Apu (Arup) and Shoma, Rita and the late Udayan Sen, Indrajit and Sandhya, Ambar and Piyali, and Parvati 'twoma' Gupta.

To Tarun, Geetan, Tiya and Cara who have journeyed with us and have been soulmates, exploring the world on this mad rollercoaster ride, sharing stories and celebrating every occasion with more than a touch of madness, creating indelible images and memories etched forever in our hearts and minds.

To our friends Manika, Prabhu, Neena, Gunjan, Viraj, Sadhana and Sudhir, for their love, support and the oh-so-delicious food served up with oodles of love and copious amounts of wine, vodka, gin and whiskey topped with rum-soaked prunes and raisins.

To my brother, Probir Roy, who took apart my first watch (the only one that I was ever gifted) to see how it worked and set us on a journey of exploration and adventure; to Sumira, my gentle and creative sister-in-law, and Ishani, Mark, Ayaan and Shivvi.

To Puneeta, my soulmate and fellow traveller who has helped heal us and make sense of this world and the other dimensions, all the while navigating our collective and individual karmas. Our grown-up lads Aditya and Avik who have taken their task of parenting and lecturing us from the age of seven a bit too seriously and have been the most fun folks to travel with to distant shores, along with our lovely daughter-in-law Parul.

To our four-legged babies who have loved us unconditionally: Choppy, Vik, Pluto, Tuggu, Khushi, Lucy, Maya, Masti and our more recent adoptions—Arth, Barfi, Dude, Ludo, the feline beauties Megh and Tara, and our soul guide and protector Puddy (Prithvi).

To our gurus and guides and to the universe for their blessings.

About the Author

Sanjoy K. Roy, an entrepreneur of the arts, is Managing Director of Teamwork Arts, which produces over thirty highly acclaimed performing arts, visual arts and literary festivals across forty cities, including the world's largest literary gathering: the annual Jaipur Literature Festival.

Roy is a founder-trustee of Salaam Baalak Trust, which provides support services for street and working children in the inner city of Delhi. He works closely with various industry bodies on important policy issues within the cultural space in India and is co-chair of the Art and Culture Committee of the Federation of Indian Chambers of Commerce and Industry; he is a former president of the Event and Entertainment Management Association and Earth Day Network's official Global Advisory Committee and is the current co-chair of Catalyst Now. He has been awarded an honorary doctorate by York University, UK.

He lives in Gurgaon with his family.

HarperCollins *Publishers* India

At HarperCollins India, we believe in telling the best stories and finding the widest readership for our books in every format possible. We started publishing in 1992; a great deal has changed since then, but what has remained constant is the passion with which our authors write their books, the love with which readers receive them, and the sheer joy and excitement that we as publishers feel in being a part of the publishing process.

Over the years, we've had the pleasure of publishing some of the finest writing from the subcontinent and around the world, including several award-winning titles and some of the biggest bestsellers in India's publishing history. But nothing has meant more to us than the fact that millions of people have read the books we published, and that somewhere, a book of ours might have made a difference.

As we look to the future, we go back to that one word—a word which has been a driving force for us all these years.

Read.